MYSTERIOUS ✦ DEATHS

Mozart

These titles are included in the *Mysterious Deaths* series:

Butch Cassidy	The Little Princes in the Tower
Amelia Earhart	Malcolm X
John F. Kennedy	Marilyn Monroe
Abraham Lincoln	Mozart

MYSTERIOUS ✦ DEATHS

Mozart

by Don Nardo

Lucent Books
P.O. Box 289011, San Diego, CA 92198-9011

Cover design: Carl Franzen

RT vⲤⲁ JH

Library of Congress Cataloging-in-Publication Data

Nardo, Don, 1947–
    Mozart / by Don Nardo.
        p. cm.—(Mysterious deaths)
    Includes bibliographical references (p.   ) and index.
    Summary: Explores the various theories surrounding the mysterious
death of Mozart at the untimely age of thirty-five.
    ISBN 1-56006-260-6 (alk. paper)
    1. Mozart, Wolfgang Amadeus, 1756–1791—Death and burial—Juvenile
literature. [1. Mozart, Wolfgang Amadeus, 1756–1791—Death and burial.]
I. Title. II. Series.
ML3930.M9N37   1997
780'.92—dc20   96-24710
[B]   CIP
                                                                                       AC MN

Printed in the U.S.A.
Copyright © 1997 by Lucent Books, Inc.
P.O. Box 289011, San Diego, CA 92198-9011

Contents

Foreword
Haunting Human History   6

Introduction
From Child Prodigy to Tragic Artist: Mozart's Life   8

Chapter 1
A Dark Figure in the Corridor: Mozart's Last Months   17

Chapter 2
*Jealousy and Dark Conspiracies: Did Someone
Poison Mozart?*   33

Chapter 3
The Medical Detectives: Did Mozart Die of Disease?   47

Chapter 4
*Between Body and Soul: Did Exhaustion
Destroy Mozart?*   58

Chapter 5
*A Kind of Emptiness: Did Mental Depression
Kill Mozart?*   68

Chapter 6
Will the Mystery of Mozart's Death Ever Be Solved?   78

For Further Reading   88

Works Consulted   90

Index   93

Picture Credits   96

About the Author   96

Haunting Human History

The *Mysterious Deaths* series focuses on nine individuals whose deaths have never been fully explained. Some are figures from the distant past; others are far more contemporary. Yet all of them remain fascinating as much for who they were and how they lived as for how they died. Their lives were characterized by fame and fortune, tragedy and triumph, secrets that led to acute vulnerability. Our enduring fascination with these stories, then, is due in part to the lives of the victims and in part to the array of conflicting facts and opinions, as well as the suspense, that surrounds their deaths.

Some of the people profiled in the *Mysterious Deaths* series were controversial political figures who lived and died in the public eye. John F. Kennedy, Abraham Lincoln, and Malcolm X were all killed in front of crowds as guards paid to protect them were unable to stop their murders. Despite all precautions, their assassins found ample opportunity to carry out their crimes. In each case, the assassins were tried and convicted. So what remains mysterious? As the reader will discover, everything.

The two women in the series, Marilyn Monroe and Amelia Earhart, are equally well remembered. Both died at the heights of their careers; both, from all appearances, had everything to live for. Yet their deaths have also been shrouded in mystery. While there are simple explanations—Monroe committed suicide, Earhart's plane crashed—the public has never been able to accept them. The more researchers dig into the deaths, the more mysterious evidence they unearth. Monroe's predilection for affairs with prominent politicians may have led to her death. Earhart, brash and cavalier, may have been involved in a government plot that collapsed around her. And these theories do not exhaust the mysterious possibilities that continue to puzzle researchers.

The circumstances of the deaths of the remaining figures in the *Mysterious Deaths* series—Richard III's nephews Edward and

Richard; the brilliant composer Wolfgang Mozart; and the infamous bank robber Butch Cassidy—are less well known but no less fascinating.

For example, what are almost surely the skeletons of the little princes Edward and Richard were found buried at the foot of a stairway in the Tower of London in 1674. To many, the discovery proved beyond a doubt that their evil uncle, Richard III, murdered them to attain the throne. Yet others find Richard wrongly accused, the obvious scapegoat. The mysterious tale of their deaths—full of dungeons, plots, and treachery—is still intriguing today.

In the history books, Wolfgang Mozart died in poverty from a consumptive-like disease. Yet there are reports and rumors, snatches of information culled from distant records, that Mozart may have died from a slow poisoning. Who could have wanted to murder the famous composer? And why?

Finally, bank robber Butch Cassidy's death couldn't have been less mysterious—shot to death by military police in Bolivia along with his companion, the Sundance Kid. Then why did members of Butch Cassidy's family and numerous others swear to have seen him, in full health, in the United States years after his supposed death?

These true-life whodunits are filled with tantalizing "what ifs?" What if Kennedy had used the bulletproof plastic hood that his Secret Servicemen had ready? What if Lincoln had decided not to attend the theater—which he did only to please his wife? What if Monroe's friend, Peter Lawford, receiving no answer to his persistent calls, had gone to her house, as he wanted to do? These questions frustrate us as well as testify to a haunting aspect of human history—the way that seemingly insignificant decisions can alter its course.

From Child Prodigy to Tragic Artist: Mozart's Life

On January 27, 1756, in the city of Salzburg, Austria, Leopold Mozart and his wife, Anna Maria, had their seventh child, Wolfgang Amadeus Mozart. The birth was an especially happy event for the Mozarts because five of their other six children had died in infancy. Young Wolfgang's only surviving sibling was his sister Maria Anna, nicknamed Nannerl, who was four years older than he. Nannerl had already shown an unusual talent for music. This delighted Leopold, since he was the assistant kapellmeister, or music director, of the orchestra sponsored by Salzburg's leading nobleman, Prince Schrattenbach, who was also the local archbishop.

Leopold was even more delighted when Wolfgang, too, gave early signs of possessing a musical gift. The proud father immersed his children in music, daily playing his violin for them and teaching them to read music even before they could read words

Eighteenth-century Salzburg, the city in which Mozart was born and spent much of his short and often tragic life.

and sentences. Both children also learned to play the harpsichord, a piano-like instrument. In 1762, when Wolfgang was only six, his father was stunned to find him composing a piece of music for the keyboard. Clearly, the boy was a prodigy, a child of rare and exceptional talent.

Mozart, age 6

Seeing a possible bright and successful future for his children, particularly Wolfgang, Leopold decided to take them on a tour of Europe's most cultured cities. By performing before rulers and other members of the nobility, he reasoned, Wolfgang and Nannerl might build a splendid artistic reputation. This was one of the few routes by which commoners like the Mozarts could hope to acquire wealth and high social position.

And so, in the autumn of 1762 the Mozart family began their first European tour with a three-week stay in Munich, the capital of Bavaria. At the time, Bavaria was one of several small German kingdoms that were loosely united in a political confederation known as the Holy Roman Empire. Besides Bavaria, some of the more important German kingdoms were Brandenburg, Prussia, and Hannover. Their leaders were royal princes who were known as "electors" because they periodically met and elected one of their number to be the Holy Roman Emperor, to oversee the entire collection of states.

For generations, the emperors had been members of the renowned Hapsburg family, which had its headquarters, the imperial court, in the Austrian capital of Vienna. As Holy Roman emperors, the Hapsburgs were by this time largely ceremonial rulers. They exerted little real control over the electors, who ran their own kingdoms more or less as they saw fit. Nevertheless, the court at Vienna, on the Danube River about 150 miles east of Salzburg, was one of the most outwardly splendid in the world. The Hapsburgs, like other European rulers, were famous for their wealth, their lavish lifestyles, and their generous patronage, or financial support, of the arts, including music.

The young Mozart performs at the piano, accompanied by his father, Leopold, and his sister, Nannerl, in Paris in 1763. The popular musical family was much in demand among European aristocrats.

It was with great eagerness, then, that Leopold Mozart took his gifted children to Vienna after their successful appearance in Munich. Sure enough, the children were an instant hit in the capital. As musicologist Michael Parouty tells it:

> The Mozarts were immediately in demand at all the best [noble] houses. They had been there barely a week when Joseph II, eldest son of the Empress Maria Theresa and future Holy Roman emperor, insisted that his mother grant the family an audience at Schonbrunn, the royal summer palace. There the empress allowed the boy to jump into her

lap, fling his arms around her neck, and give her a big kiss. The entire court was enraptured by the confident little boy for whom nothing seemed too difficult.

Reactions were similar in Brussels, Cologne, and every other city the Mozarts visited. In Paris, the French royal family invited the children to perform at the palace of Versailles, the largest and most lavish royal residence in all of Europe.

On this and later trips to Europe's great cities, young Wolfgang Mozart met many of the greatest musicians of the day, some of whom influenced his composing style. For example, in London he met Johann Christian Bach, the youngest son of the famous composer Johann Sebastian Bach. The younger Bach not only had a profound effect on Mozart's music, but also became one of his closest friends. Other important composers in the middle years of the eighteenth century were Franz Joseph Haydn, Christoph Willibald Gluck, and Johann Adolf Hasse, who said of the young Mozart, "One day this child will eclipse us all."

Indeed, Mozart got off to an early and spectacular start as a composer. As he grew older, he became known less as a performer and more as a composer who could turn out lovely pieces with

Mozart and Nannerl perform for Empress Maria Theresa. The members of the court were surprised and charmed when the little boy jumped into the empress's lap and kissed her.

Johann Christian Bach

amazing ease and quickness. In those days, various nobles and church leaders regularly commissioned, or hired, people to write music for weddings, funerals, coronations, important parties, and so on. And each royal court had its own orchestra and singers who performed both religious works and popular operas. Mozart received his first commissions at the age of eleven and a year later wrote his first opera, *The Sly Maiden*. This work was performed in 1769 in Salzburg to celebrate the archbishop's birthday.

Also in 1769, the thirteen-year-old Mozart traveled to Italy, where the light, jovial music of the Italian composers strongly influenced his writing. In the following three years, he frequently traveled back and forth from Austria to Italy. During that time he composed at least six symphonies, long pieces for full orchestra, as well as the operas *Mithridates, King of Pontus*, and *Lucio Silla*, and many shorter works.

Despite his frequent commissions and fame as a performer, Mozart did not achieve the financial security he and his father had envisioned. This was largely because the younger Mozart was a poor money manager who quickly spent whatever he made. Thus, as he grew into manhood he found it increasingly difficult to make ends meet and often relied on funds borrowed from family and friends. To achieve financial security, he

Mozart, age 13

tried desperately to find a permanent important musical post such as official court composer or kapellmeister. But such coveted jobs were few and the competition for them was heavy. Thus, to pay the bills Mozart eventually had to begin giving music lessons, which he considered a boring waste of time.

On May 19, 1789, Mozart appears at a Berlin performance of his opera, The Abduction from the Seraglio.

In January 1779, at age twenty-three, Mozart finally achieved a modest permanent position—that of composer and organist for the archbishop of Salzburg. While in this post he composed the magnificent opera *Idomeneo* at the request of the elector of Bavaria. But only two years later, Mozart, a headstrong and temperamental young man, had a falling-out with the archbishop and resigned his position.

Turning his back on Salzburg, Mozart journeyed to Vienna in hopes of gaining the job of official composer at the imperial court. But he was passed over, this time in favor of the less talented Italian composer Antonio Salieri. But Mozart did manage to get an important commission to write an opera, *The Abduction from the Seraglio*, for a local theater. One of his greatest works, it opened in

July 1782 and enjoyed much popularity with the public. However, after seeing the opera, Joseph II, now Holy Roman Emperor and the man whom Mozart most wanted to impress, reacted with the inane statement, "Too many notes, my dear Mozart."

Helping to make up for this disappointment was Mozart's courtship of and marriage to a young Viennese woman, Constanze Weber, in that same year. Despite constant financial troubles and

A 1782 portrait of Constanze Weber, the Viennese woman whom Mozart married on August 4, 1782, at St. Stephen's Cathedral in Vienna.

the deaths of four children in infancy, the couple enjoyed a close, loving relationship and a lasting marriage. Their two surviving children, Karl Thomas and Franz Wolfgang Xaver, were born in 1784 and 1791, respectively.

Mozart's happy marriage was all the more remarkable considering that his life and fortunes seemed to spiral relentlessly downward in the following years. Having been frail and sickly all his life, he was frequently ill. And compounding his poor health was a growing tendency to worry not only about money, but also about how people perceived his music. His 1786 opera *The Marriage of Figaro* was far too novel and sophis-

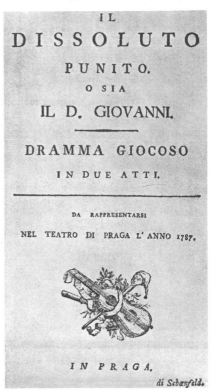

IL
DISSOLUTO
PUNITO.
O SIA
IL D. GIOVANNI.
——
DRAMMA GIOCOSO
IN DUE ATTI.

DA RAPPRESENTARSI
NEL TEATRO DI PRAGA L'ANNO 1787.

IN PRAGA.
di Schœnfeld.

The title page of the first edition of the libretto to Don Giovanni.

ticated for Viennese audiences at the time and received only a lukewarm reception. The following year, his *Don Giovanni*, now considered one of the greatest operas ever written, flopped in Vienna. Also in 1787, Leopold Mozart died, leaving his son emotionally devastated.

In less than twenty years Mozart had undergone a sad transformation from child prodigy of amazing potential to tragic artist with a bleak and unsure future. In 1790, with his health steadily deteriorating and his financial problems turning from bad to worse, he searched desperately for steady work in the music field. Joseph II had recently died, and the composer applied to the new emperor, Leopold II, for the position of assistant kapellmeister. Mozart was rejected for the job, however, and was so poor that he had to turn down a commission for two new operas because he could not afford to travel to Britain, where the patron resided. In 1791 he worked on a new opera, *The Magic Flute*, and a requiem, a musical setting of the mass for the dead. Ironically, the religious

Mozart lies near death on December 4, 1791. In the early hours of December 5, he passed away, leaving behind a mystery that still persists.

composition seemed to portend his own untimely death. The period in which he struggled to write the piece, a commission he received under very strange circumstances, proved to be the mysterious and very controversial final months of his life.

1 A Dark Figure in the Corridor: Mozart's Last Months

The exact circumstances of Mozart's strange death are difficult to determine. This is because no single person made a detailed record of the events of the last few months of his life, in order, as they happened. Only later, over the course of the following months, years, and decades, did various people who knew the composer set down their memories of his last months on earth. These accounts became the foundation for the following version

Frequently ill and depressed, Mozart rarely looked as healthy and happy as this portrait depicts him.

of this period, the popular and romantic story that became the most widely accepted and was most often quoted.

A Veil of Secrecy

The first strange incident in Mozart's last year, 1791, occurred in July, about five months before his death. It was at this time that he received a commission to compose a requiem mass, a piece that would later prove to be the most controversial of all his works. Part of the controversy involves the way the *Requiem* itself affected Mozart. In that fateful last year of his life, this mass for the dead seemed both to consume his attention and to drain him emotionally.

Even more controversial are the odd and secretive circumstances under which Mozart received the commission for the work that July. One of the first people who described these circumstances was Franz Niemetschek, a German teacher and writer who authored an early biography of the composer. According to Niemetschek, one dreary July night Mozart, who was not expecting a caller, heard a slow and powerful knocking on his door. His body weak and his complexion pale from nearly constant sickness, the composer shuffled to the door. What he saw when he opened it briefly caused his face to lose even more of its color, for standing in the corridor was a strange man dressed in a long cloak that concealed his entire body.

For a moment the two men stared at each other in silence. When the stranger finally spoke he did so in serious and somber tones

An Irreplaceable Loss

On December 6, 1791, the day of Mozart's burial, the following obituary appeared in the widely read Vienna newspaper the Wiener Zeitung.

"Wolfgang Mozart died during the night of December 4–5. From childhood on he was known throughout Europe for his most exceptional musical talent. Through the successful development and diligent application of his extraordinary natural gifts, he scaled the heights of the greatest masters. His works, which are loved and admired everywhere, are proof of his greatness—and they reveal the irreplaceable loss which the noble art of music has suffered through his death."

that made Mozart feel even less at ease. The man, who refused to identify himself, claimed to be a messenger from a music patron who also preferred to remain anonymous. After this mysterious introduction, the messenger presented the surprised composer with an unsigned letter filled with flattering praises for the beauty of his music. The letter asked whether Mozart would consider writing a mass for the dead and also inquired what fee he would require and how long the composing would take. Unnerved by the unusual manner of these requests, Mozart told the visitor he needed to think it over. The visitor replied that this was acceptable, gave Mozart an address to write to, and abruptly departed, leaving the frail and astonished composer standing in his open doorway.

Wolfgang and Constanze Mozart

Mozart immediately went to Constanze, who had not overheard the conversation in the corridor, and explained what had happened. According to Niemetschek, the composer, who never acted without consulting his wife, "told her about the strange commission, and expressed his desire also to try his hand at this genre [style], especially since his genius was always ideally suited to the lofty and dramatic style of church music." During the conversation, the two wondered aloud about who this mysterious patron was and why he or she wanted to remain anonymous. Also, who was the messenger who had displayed such a dark air of mystery, both in his dress and in his grim manner? It all seemed very odd. Yet, Constanze pointed out, Mozart had admitted to his interest in composing a requiem mass. And more importantly, the patron who chose to hide behind a veil of secrecy seemed perfectly willing to pay. Since the Mozart family was desperately in need of money, Constanze advised her husband to accept the commission.

Mozart agreed with his wife. As Niemetschek told it, he promptly

> wrote back to the unknown patron, saying he would compose the requiem for a certain fee. . . . Shortly thereafter the same messenger appeared, bringing not only the

stipulated [agreed upon] fee, but also . . . the promise of a considerable bonus upon receipt of the work. [Mozart] . . . should make no attempt to discover the identity of his patron, as his efforts would surely be in vain.

A Kiss and a Thunderous Ovation

As time went on, the strange messenger appeared again and again. And each time, the composer became more agitated, more fearful of not pleasing his unknown benefactor, and more obsessed with finding out that benefactor's identity. One of the messenger's unexpected appearances occurred in early September 1791 as the Mozarts were departing for the city of Prague to attend the coronation of the new king of Bohemia. In the preceding month, Mozart had found little time or energy to work on the commissioned mass. He felt guilty, since he had already taken money for the job. And he hoped the ominous messenger would not notice that the Mozarts were taking this trip, which obviously would further delay completion of the work.

But in this regard the composer's hopes were in vain. As the couple climbed into their carriage to leave for Prague, the cloaked figure suddenly emerged from the night mists and tugged at Constanze's skirt. "What will now become of the requiem?" the phantom inquired. The startled Mozart apologized profusely for

Mozart at work in his study in Vienna. Here, in 1791, as he became increasingly ill, he composed The Magic Flute, *his last opera.*

Die

Zauberflöte.

Eine
Oper in drei Aufzügen,
neubearbeitet

von

C. A. Vulpius.

Die Musik ist von Mozart.

Aufgeführt auf dem Herzoglichen Hoftheater zu
Weimar zum erstenmal am
16. Januar 1794.

Leipzig, 1794,
bei Johann Samuel Heinsius.

Papageno.

The frontpiece of the first edition of The Magic Flute, *showing one of the characters—Papageno, a bird catcher (left).*

the delays. He promised to work diligently on the mass as soon as he returned from Prague and stated that he hoped to complete the work within four weeks. Seemingly satisfied, the dark figure spun around and hurried back into the concealing mists.

But Mozart had spoken without thinking. He had not yet finished *The Magic Flute*, which was set to open on September 30, only a few weeks hence. Despite his promise to the messenger, therefore, he felt he had no choice but to devote most of his time to completing the opera. These were harrowing weeks for the composer. He had been feeling exhausted and sick for months and now the pressure of finishing the opera on time, combined with worry over the unfinished mass, seemed to worsen his condition.

Yet when *The Magic Flute* had its first performances at a Vienna theater beginning on the last day of September, the composer's spirits lifted noticeably, if only briefly. The crowd was made up of local townspeople, most of them commoners and many of moderate or little means. This group contrasted sharply with the audiences that frequented the concerts presented at the imperial court. While many of the wealthy and noble members of the court audiences had not understood or appreciated Mozart's last few operas, these ordinary folk thoroughly enjoyed *The Magic Flute*. Their enthusiastic reactions made the first few nights of the opera's run among the most fulfilling of the composer's life.

Typical was opening night. Mozart, too weak to stand for any length of time, conducted while sitting at the keyboard. His trusted and gifted music pupil, Franz Süssmayer, turned the pages of the music score for him. A foretaste of the audience's reception of the piece occurred in the moment of silence following the overture, or introductory music. A young composer named Johann Schenk was so moved by what he had heard that he crawled up to the pianoforte and kissed Mozart's hand. The outpouring of love for Mozart continued. At the conclusion of the performance, he was overjoyed at hearing the spectators' thunderous ovation and cries of "Bravo!" And he was deeply touched when the audience demanded encores, or repetitions, of some of the songs.

"One Cannot Change One's Destiny"

Mozart wanted desperately to conduct all the performances of the new opera. Because of his frail condition, however, he could manage this only for one more night. The theater's kapellmeister took over the strenuous task in the weeks that followed, although the composer did manage to attend most of the performances. As was his habit, he shared his joy with Constanze, who, because of an illness of her own, was attending a health spa in the town of Baden, a few miles south of Vienna. They were so close that they corresponded almost daily when apart, and on October 9 he wrote to her:

Constanze Mozart

Dearest, Most Beloved Little Wife,

I was exceedingly delighted and overjoyed to find your letter on my return from the opera. [On] Saturday . . . the opera was performed to a full house with the usual applause and repetition of numbers. It will be given again tomorrow. . . . By the way, you have no idea how charming the music sounds when you hear it from a box [small compartment of private seats projecting from the theater's side wall] close to the orchestra—it sounds much better than from the gallery. As soon as you return, you must try this for yourself. . . . Farewell, my love—I kiss you millions of times and am ever your

Mozart

In this and other letters to Constanze during September and early October, Mozart rarely mentioned the state of his own health. Though he was concerned about his condition, he was more concerned about his wife's and felt it best not to worry her during her recovery at the health spa. So he did not tell her that in addition to feeling weak and suffering from bouts of depression he was increasingly beset by headaches, muscle pains, fever, and nausea. Often, he lay awake at night wondering what was wrong with him. Was it disease or perhaps exhaustion?

Antonio Salieri

Or maybe someone was slowly poisoning him. But who, he asked himself, could hate him enough to want to see him dead? In the past, he had had disagreements with some of his patrons, such as the archbishop of Salzburg, but none of these incidents had been serious enough to warrant a reprisal as extreme as murder. Then there were the occasional rumors that other composers were jealous of Mozart's great talent. Indeed, Antonio Salieri, the man who had been appointed instead of Mozart as imperial composer, had on a number of occasions kept the emperor from hearing some of Mozart's best pieces. Was this out of jealousy? Even if it was, Mozart reasoned, it seemed outlandish that a man of Salieri's position would stoop to murder.

Searching for another theory for his illness, Mozart turned to a divine explanation. Perhaps God was punishing him for making such a mess of his finances, or for taking too much pride in his

An Eternal Peace

Shortly after her husband's death, Constanze Mozart expressed her undying affection for him by writing the following entry in the album in which he kept signed messages and letters from his closest friends. On September 3, 1787, Mozart had written a touching farewell to his recently deceased friend and former doctor, Sigmund Barisani, and Constanze chose to write her own farewell to her husband on the back of that same page.

"What you once wrote to your friend on this page, do I now in my affliction write to you, dearly beloved husband; Mozart—never to be forgotten by me or by the whole of Europe—now you too are at peace—eternal peace!! About one o'clock in the morning of the 5th of December in this year he left in his 36th year—alas! all too soon!—this good—but ungrateful world!—dear God!—For 8 years we were joined together by the most tender bond, never to be broken here below [on earth]!—O! Could I soon be joined with you forever [in heaven],

Your grievously afflicted wife
Constanze Mozart *née Weber*"

Constanze Mozart in a portrait painted in 1802, about eleven years after her husband's death.

music, or for some other reason the sick man could not fathom. The only thing he was certain of was the constant, gnawing, frightening feeling that his life was steadily ebbing away. In a letter to a musical colleague, he wrote:

> I have come to the end before having enjoyed my talent. Life was so lovely, my career opened under such happy conditions, but one cannot change one's destiny. No one can know the measure of his days; one must resign oneself, for it will all go as Providence [God's will] decrees. I end my days; here is my requiem which I must not leave unfinished.

The Unwanted Caller

In fact, the unfinished requiem mass remained on Mozart's mind all through the rehearsals and early performances of *The Magic Flute*, while Constanze was away at the spa and he was alone in the small Vienna apartment, unhappy to be facing a crisis without his wife's support. He was sure that a crisis was in the making, for the four weeks allotted for the completion of the mass were almost up and he had done very little work on the piece. Consequently, he dreaded his next meeting with the messenger. Just thinking about that slow and demanding pounding on the door and that dark and ominous figure in the corridor made the composer shiver.

Sure enough, on the very day the four weeks were up, a powerful and deliberate knocking reverberated through Mozart's rooms. Trembling from a combination of his illness and sheer nervous anticipation, he slowly approached the door. Then he hesitated. There was always the possibility that if he remained quiet and pretended not to be at home the unwanted caller might go away. But would he stay away? Even if the ruse worked today, the composer reasoned, the messenger would surely come back. He would return again and again, growing angrier on each trip, until he cornered the composer and demanded the finished mass. Deciding that it would be better to face the consequences sooner than later, Mozart gathered his courage, drew a deep breath, and opened the door. There, confirming his fears, stood the dark figure.

After an awkward pause, Mozart broke the silence. "I could not keep to my word," he admitted meekly. He half expected the messenger to bellow in rage, or even to strike him. But to his surprise the man did not seem angry.

Mozart's study, in which he worked on the Requiem.

"I know you couldn't," the visitor responded. "You were right not to force yourself. The quality of the work might have suffered. How long will you require now?"

Mozart thought about it for several seconds, then blurted out, "Another four weeks! The work has become more and more interesting to me." This claim was true, for Mozart had become increasingly intrigued by the possibilities a mass presented for expressing majestic, emotional, and moving musical themes. Then still fearful, he embellished the truth with a lie. "I am expanding it more than I wished to do at first. Four more weeks should be sufficient." Would the man accept this halfhearted offer? Mozart wondered.

"Good," said the messenger, much to Mozart's relief. Suddenly, the caller began to reach inside his cloak, causing the composer to tense up once again. What new and perhaps unwanted surprise would the fellow produce from beneath his all-concealing garment? Would it be another letter from the mysterious patron? Or perhaps it would be a club, a knife, or some other weapon with which to scare the composer into working harder and faster.

"But you must be paid more, too," said the man. He handed the surprised Mozart a small leather purse and added "Here is another hundred ducats."

"Sir," the bewildered composer asked timidly, "who is it that has sent you?"

"As you have already been told, the man wished to remain anonymous," was the stern reply.

"Who are *you*, then," inquired Mozart, surprised at his own boldness.

"That is even less to the point. In four weeks I shall come back to you." And with that, the messenger turned and disappeared into the dark shadows of the stairwell, once more leaving Mozart standing alone in his open doorway. After a few seconds the composer had an idea. Quickly, he gathered together whatever coins he could find in the apartment and rushed downstairs. There, he handed the money to some neighbor children and asked them to follow the cloaked stranger, who was still in sight at the end of the street. In this stealthy way, Mozart hoped to discover the identity of both the messenger and the man he claimed to work for.

A Phantom from Beyond?

A few days later, on October 16, Constanze, who was feeling much better, returned from the Baden spa. Although her husband had not disclosed to her the full extent of his deteriorating health, she had learned of it from relatives and friends. Extremely concerned, she immediately took charge of the family's affairs and did her best to care for her husband and see to his everyday needs while he attempted, in his increasingly feeble state, to work on his music.

Shortly after Constanze's return, Mozart related the messenger's latest appearance. After giving the matter much serious thought, he said, he had come to a momentous conclusion. The patron the messenger represented was no mortal person, but rather, some divine being, perhaps God himself, which meant that the messenger was also not of this earth. Indeed, ranted the ailing composer, he had paid people to follow the messenger. Yet although they had kept the man in sight and stayed on his trail, he had simply vanished without a trace. Did this not prove that he was truly a phantom

Mozart and his family occupied an apartment in 1791 in this corner house on the Viennese thoroughfare called Rauhensteingasse.

from beyond? Thus, declared Mozart, the commission of a requiem must be an announcement, a divine warning of his own impending death. God or one of God's agents must be instructing the composer to produce a religious mass to commemorate his own passing! In spite of Constanze's doubts about this interpretation of the commission, Mozart continued to believe it. He was determined, no matter how sick he became, to produce a musical work worthy of the divine forces that had commissioned it.

And so, in mid-October Mozart threw himself into the arduous task of finishing the *Requiem*. This time, he promised himself, he would meet the new deadline he and the phantom messenger had agreed upon. But he had no sooner devoted himself to the task when another important job materialized. A friend, the well-known clarinettist Anton Stadler, begged Mozart to compose a clarinet concerto, a work for that instrument and full orchestra. This would entail frequent visits by Stadler to the Mozart residence to check on the composer's progress. Mozart wondered why Stadler, who knew full well that Mozart was deathly ill, was so insistent on having his clarinet piece right away. But the composer

The ailing Mozart, accompanied by his pupil, Franz Süssmayer, and several musicians, does his best to sing sections of his still unfinished Requiem.

had never been able to refuse a friend a favor, and this request was no exception. In the following weeks he worked nearly night and day on both the concerto and the *Requiem,* often fainting from exhaustion and then resuming work as soon as he regained consciousness.

Mozart finished the Clarinet Concerto first and then continued to work feverishly on the *Requiem.* He was confident that the divine messenger was able to monitor his progress from afar and would not return until the work was finished. But the herculean working pace the composer had imposed on his own frail body was too much to bear. By November 20, he could no longer stand up, let alone walk, and Constanze confined him to his bed. Soon, his hands and feet began to swell painfully. As other parts of his body began to swell, he found that he could no longer turn in bed and his wife had to help him with eating, washing, and other everyday functions.

The Taste of Death

In spite of his pitiful physical condition, Mozart insisted on completing the *Requiem.* When he became too exhausted to write, or when his fingers were too swollen to hold a pen, he dictated the musical notes to his pupil Süssmayer, who sat by the bedside. Meanwhile, Mozart grew increasingly weaker. His physician, Thomas Closset, came by periodically, examined him, and placed cold compresses on his forehead. Dr. Closset declared that Mozart was suffering from a severe fever brought on by unknown causes and seemed convinced that the illness would pass in time. But as the days wore on the composer's condition only worsened. By the beginning of December Constanze was so worried about her husband that she sent for her sister Sophie to help her take care of him.

"Thank God you have come, dear Sophie," Constanze said tearfully as her sister entered the apartment on the morning of December 4. "Last night he was so ill that I did not think he would be alive this morning. I fear that if he has another bad turn he will not survive the night. Go to him for a while and see for yourself how ill he is."

When Sophie entered the bedroom she was appalled by the sight of her brother-in-law's pale, swollen body. Managing to hold back the tears for his sake, she went to the bed and carefully took

In this somewhat fanciful painting, done long after Mozart's death, the composer's family and friends surround his deathbed, where he valiantly struggles to finish the Requiem.

his hand. "Ah, dear Sophie," he said. "How glad I am that you have come. You must stay here tonight and see me die." Sophie insisted that he would not die, that his health would eventually improve and he would be his old self again. But he only shook his head. "Why, I already have the taste of death on my tongue," he said.

After consoling Mozart a while longer, Sophie left to arrange for a priest to come in case the dying man needed the last rites. When she returned, she found the composer, who believed himself to be near death, instructing Süssmayer on how to finish the *Requiem*. That evening, Dr. Closset paid another visit and once more applied cold compresses to his patient's forehead and also to his chest. However, these measures did not help. With Constanze, Sophie, Süssmayer, and Closset at his bedside, Mozart drifted in and out of consciousness. Outside, a violent storm raged, and it occurred to some of those present that nature was marking the passing of a genius.

Shortly after midnight, in the early hours of December 5, Mozart awakened long enough to make one last desperate and heroic effort to finish the *Requiem*. "His last movement was an attempt to express with his mouth the drum passage in the *Requiem*," Sophie later recalled. "That I can still hear." A few moments later, the thirty-five-year-old Mozart closed his eyes for the last time and Dr. Closset declared him dead. At this, Constanze threw herself on her knees and in loud sobs called upon God to care for her beloved husband in heaven. She then remained steadfastly beside his body for the rest of the night and all through the next day as a large number of family friends and Mozart's colleagues came to pay their last respects.

As it turned out, these visits constituted a more fitting final memorial to the composer than his funeral. Close friends advised Constanze that because she and her husband had been so poor, she would have to be content with the cheapest possible funeral. He would have to be buried in a "pauper's grave," an unmarked cemetery plot containing the bodies of dozens of impoverished individuals. Adding to Constanze's grief, the few friends who tried to attend the burial were thwarted by another bout of violent weather. According to a local innkeeper:

A cart bears Mozart's casket in this nineteenth-century drawing. According to tradition, he was buried in a pauper's grave.

At the funeral . . . it began to rage and storm. Rain and snow fell at the same time, as if Nature wanted to show her anger with the great composer's contemporaries, who had turned out extremely sparsely for his burial. Only a few friends and three women accompanied the corpse. . . . As the storm grew ever more violent, even these friends determined to turn back.

And so, the man who would one day be hailed as one of the greatest artists in history reached his last and forever unmarked resting place utterly alone. Of his tumultuous life, one marked by both triumph and tragedy, much was known. Yet the cause or causes of his untimely death remained shrouded in mystery.

2 Jealousy and Dark Conspiracies: Did Someone Poison Mozart?

As it turned out, Mozart achieved much more success in death than in life. He left behind an enormous legacy of wonderful musical works, and he is now recognized as one of the world's greatest composers. But he also left behind a baffling puzzle. How exactly did he die? Over the years, a number of theories for his demise, some of them mundane, others strange, romantic, and sensational, were proposed. On the mundane side were the claims that repeated bouts with serious illness had finally caused his frail body to cease functioning; or that the composer, a known workaholic, had driven himself to a state of extreme exhaustion that proved to be fatal. More exotic were reports of death due to undiagnosed kidney disease or at the hands of his doctors, who had in good faith used treatments seen today as primitive and dangerous. And more ominous were the suggestions that the composer was poisoned, either by a jealous colleague or as part of a large-scale conspiracy.

Mozart, age 35

As each new theory either contradicted or combined with the others, fact and legend slowly and steadily blurred together. As a result, to this very day the exact circumstances surrounding the death of one of the world's best loved artists remain mysterious and controversial. And the "romantic version" of his last months, featuring his fear of the dark messenger, his pauper's burial, and so on, is still the one generally familiar to the public. In recent years a number of scholars have reexamined the various theories, but no clear consensus has emerged. Responsible investigation, however, indicates that much of the supposed evidence offered in support of many of the theories is hearsay, exaggeration, or both. Such examinations also call into question the accuracy of much in the romantic version of the composer's death.

Stirring Up Foul Play

The idea that someone poisoned Mozart, perhaps the most popular and widely accepted of all the theories for his demise, is a case in point. Was there any solid evidence that the composer died of poisoning? Or did the theory become widely popular simply because it was more dramatic and intriguing than the others?

The official cause of death registered in December 1791 by Mozart's attending physician, Thomas Closset, was "severe fever accompanied by a rash." This explanation was, more or less, accepted by Mozart's colleagues and by the public for several years after the composer's passing. But not everyone, it seems, was satisfied with the vague pronouncement. Fever and rash, after all, are symptoms of illness, not illnesses in themselves. The same is true of swelling of the body parts, a symptom no one disputed that Mozart had exhibited in his last days. The fact is that any one of a wide range of diseases and physical conditions could have produced these symptoms. One such condition results from poisoning. Less than a month after Mozart's death, a reporter for a Berlin newspaper published the following report:

> Mozart is—dead. . . . Because his body swelled up after death, some people believe that he was poisoned. . . . Now that he is dead the Viennese will at last realize what they have lost in him. In his life he was constantly the object of cabals [plots against him], which he at times may well have provoked by his *sans souci* [tactless and irresponsible] manner.

It is impossible to be certain of the identity of the "some people" alluded to by the reporter. But there is evidence suggesting that some members of Mozart's family believed their famous relative had been poisoned. For example, his son Karl Thomas later wrote a note that stated in part, "Another indicative circumstance [piece of evidence] is that the body did not become stiff and cold, but

Mozart's son, Karl Thomas, who made his living in government administration, remained a lifelong bachelor and died childless.

remained soft and elastic in all parts, as was the case with Pope Ganganelli [Clement XIV, who died in 1774] and others who died of organic poisons." However, Karl Thomas Mozart did not publish or widely discuss his suspicion. Perhaps this was because he was not all that sure of it. Or maybe he concluded that stirring up a controversy about foul play would unduly upset his mother and other relatives. In any case, the reporter's newspaper blurb also went largely unnoticed, and for a while most people just accepted the "fever" version of Mozart's death.

A Growing Mythology

In 1798 Niemetschek published the first major book about Mozart. According to this biographer, Mozart believed not only that he was writing the *Requiem* to commemorate his own impending death, but also that he was being slowly poisoned by the unknown agent or agents who had commissioned the piece. Niemetschek claimed to have gotten this information from Constanze Mozart herself.

Supposedly, she had tried early on to convince her husband that his suspicions about poisoning were wrong. But she did suspect the existence of some sort of conspiracy against him and came to believe that he had been right about poisoning after all.

Niemetschek was not specific about who was behind the alleged murder. Without naming names, however, he hinted that the "Italian composers" of the day hated and envied Mozart and might have wanted to see him dead. Supposedly, Constanze herself suspected the Italians. One reason for Niemetschek's failure to be specific was his lack of a primary source; that is, he did not get his information directly from his subject. The writer had never interviewed Mozart; indeed, the two had met only once, on the occasion of a performance of one of the composer's operas early in 1791. To write his book, then, Niemetschek attempted to piece together the events of his subject's life from interviews with the composer's relatives and friends and from documents written by Mozart and about him. Many of these materials were sketchy, and sometimes they contradicted one another; in retrospect, it is possible to question some of the biographer's allegations and conclusions.

Title page of Niemetschek's 1798 biography of Mozart.

Despite its shortcomings, Niemetschek's book was an important milestone because it ignited a sudden burst of popularity for the suggestion that Mozart had died of poisoning. Many other writers, including Friedrich Rochlitz, the editor of a popular German musical journal, published their own versions of Mozartian foul play. Year after year, anecdotes about Mozart's life and death appeared in books and articles. Many of these tales were based on descriptions and speculations by other writers, Niemetschek for one, rather than on original documents, interviews, and other factual accounts. To Niemetschek's credit, he had tried his best to establish the validity of his sources. Many of the less thorough writers who followed him tended only to inflate and embellish a growing mythology about the composer's last months.

The Phantoms Revealed

The mythology concerning the death of Mozart included increasingly dramatic and detailed descriptions of the visits by the mysterious messenger and some elaborations on the idea that the anonymous patron was poisoning the artist he had hired. Some accounts, including that of Rochlitz, even provided specific dialogue between Mozart and the cloaked visitor. In fact, no one witnessed most of the meetings between Mozart and the patron's agent. And the composer left behind few, if any, indications in his letters of the specific content of the conversations. Therefore, almost all the ominous details surrounding the "phantom" messenger were the invention of later writers seeking to capitalize on the popularity of the Mozartian mystery.

To be sure, there *was* a messenger who did in fact represent an anonymous patron. Indeed, the identity of Mozart's benefactor was revealed shortly after the composer's death, a fact that the more sensational writers either did not know or chose to ignore. As Volkmar Braunbehrens explains in his book *Mozart in Vienna:*

> The patron was Count Franz Walsegg-Stuppach, who . . . was a music lover who played both flute and cello and gave chamber music soirées [parties] at his home twice a week. . . . It is said that he had the peculiar habit of asking his guests to guess who had written the music they had just heard; when they flattered him with the suggestion that he might be the composer, he gave a meaningful smile and gave no denial. . . . In any event, he ordered the *Requiem* as a memorial to his wife, Anna, who had died . . . in February 1791.

Though the messenger's identity is less certain, a number of reputable scholars have suggested that he was Walsegg's steward, Franz Lietgeb. Interestingly, in the one portrait that has been authenticated, Lietgeb *does* display a somewhat grim and sinister appearance.

Among several of Mozart's friends who knew that Count Walsegg was the secret patron was the musician Abbé Maximilian Stadler, who wrote in an 1826 letter:

> I learned just after Mozart's death that Count Walsegg had ordered the *Requiem*. I also knew all along about the count's

Abbé Maximilian Stadler

plans and everything else that was kept secret. . . . But as it is improper and forbidden to reveal secrets [about friends and loved ones], I never once permitted myself to reveal the patron's name.

It is uncertain exactly when Constanze Mozart learned about Walsegg. But there is little doubt that she eventually did. Süssmayer finished the *Requiem*, and Constanze saw to it that it was delivered to the patron. In December 1793 Count Walsegg conducted the piece in public. Constanze then tried to publish the *Requiem* and the count threatened a lawsuit, claiming that he had paid for the piece and was therefore its sole owner. He and Constanze eventually agreed on an out-of-court financial settlement.

The proof that the unknown patron and his messenger were neither phantoms nor divine agents explodes part of the mythology surrounding the final months of Mozart's life. It also eliminates one of the more romantic and popular suspects in the supposed poisoning of the composer. Walsegg had not the slightest motive for killing Mozart. Indeed, the count desperately wanted to see the *Requiem* finished and would have been defeating his own purpose by poisoning the creator of the work.

Consumed by Jealousy

A seemingly more likely murder suspect surfaced in 1823. In that year former imperial court composer Antonio Salieri, now an old man, attempted suicide by cutting his throat. The attempt failed and Salieri lived for another year and a half, although very ill and emotionally depressed. Meanwhile, the word spread far and wide that he had confessed to having poisoned Mozart. Many people apparently believed these rumors, including the great German composer Ludwig van Beethoven, who, in his journal, reported a colleague as saying:

Salieri is very ill again. He is quite deranged. In his ravings he keeps claiming that he is guilty of Mozart's death and made away with [killed] him by poison. This is the truth, for he wants to make a confession of it, so it is true once again that everything has its reward [people are ultimately punished for their crimes].

The last two pages written in Mozart's own hand of his score for the Requiem.

Justice Does Not Exist

Russia's Aleksandr Pushkin was the first writer to dramatize the idea that Antonio Salieri killed Mozart out of professional jealousy. In this speech, from Pushkin's short play Mozart and Salieri, *Salieri laments what he sees as divine injustice. The Italian composer has dedicated his entire life to the art of music. He has worked hard and followed the rules, yet God has chosen to impart the gift of genius to the carefree and irresponsible Mozart, for whom composing great music comes as easily as breathing.*

"SALIERI: Justice, they say, does not exist on earth.
But justice won't be found in heaven either:
That's plain as any simple [musical] scale to me.
Born with a love of art, when as a child
I heard the lofty organ sound, I listened,
I listened and the sweet tears freely flowed.
Early in life I turned from vain amusements;
All studies that did not accord with music
I loathed, despised, rejected out of hand;
I gave myself to music. Hard as were
The earliest steps, and dull the earliest path,
I rose above reverses. Craftsmanship I took to be a
    pedestal of art:
I made myself a craftsman, gave my fingers
Obedient, arid virtuosity [technical skill]. . . .
I envy—I profoundly envy. Heaven!
O where is justice when the sacred gift,
Immortal genius, comes not in reward
For toil, devotion, prayer, self-sacrifice—
But shines instead inside a mad-
    cap's [impulsive person's] skull,
An idle hooligan's? O Mozart,
    Mozart!"

Aleksandr Pushkin (1799–1837), the popular and influential Russian author of Eugene Onegin *and* Boris Godunov, *as well as* Mozart and Salieri.

Antonio Salieri, who was appointed court composer in Vienna in 1774, was rumored to have confessed to killing Mozart.

The most important element missing from Salieri's controversial rumored confession was a motive for the crime. Popular writers quickly provided that motive. For example, in 1830, only five years after Salieri's death, the renowned Russian writer Aleksandr Pushkin wrote the one-act play *Mozart and Salieri*. In his dramatization, Pushkin suggested that the Italian composer was consumed by jealousy because he realized that he could never write music as great as Mozart's. Frustrated and angry that God would grant such magnificent talent and genius to an "idle hooligan," Salieri supposedly poisoned his hated rival by slow stages.

The idea that Salieri killed Mozart because of professional jealousy was so intriguing, dramatic, and romantic that it quickly became the most popular theory for Mozart's death. And it inspired many later dramatizations. In 1898 the Russian composer Nikolay Rimsky-Korsakov turned Pushkin's play into an opera, also titled *Mozart and Salieri*, that enjoyed wide popularity in Europe. This opera, in turn, became the major basis for British playwright Peter Shaffer's full-length 1979 play, *Amadeus*. Shaffer's play won a number of theater awards in Britain and the United States and inspired the 1984 feature film of the same name that won the Academy Award for best picture. All these versions of the story depicted Salieri as a weak man of minimal talent, driven by overwhelming feelings of jealousy to commit an unspeakable crime.

But did Salieri actually do it? The fact is that this tremendously popular and widely accepted theory has no documented evidence to back it up. The only damning points against Salieri consist of hearsay and conjecture. It *has* been documented that the Italian did his level best to keep the emperor from hearing Mozart's music and also that he criticized Mozart in private conversations. But such behavior in itself is hardly enough to justify a charge of murder. Constanze Mozart, who suspected the Italian composer's involvement in her husband's death, eventually told some writer friends that Salieri must be guilty. But she offered no proof, and it is certainly possible that she was just offering her support for the increasingly popular view.

Moreover, some evidence exists that Salieri *did not* kill his musical rival. First, a pianist and former pupil of Salieri's visited the former court composer in the hospital in 1823 and later recorded:

> The reunion was a sad one; for his appearance shocked me, and he spoke only in broken sentences of his approaching death; but finally with the words: "Although this is my last illness, however I assure you in good faith that there is no truth in the absurd rumor; you know what I mean—that I poisoned Mozart. But no . . . tell the world that it is malice, pure malice; old Salieri, who will soon be dead, has told you this."

Also, Salieri's friend Giuseppe Carpani, who was disturbed about the rumors claiming that his compatriot was a murderer, conducted an investigation. Carpani interviewed the two nurses who had attended Salieri after his suicide attempt. They signed a declaration stating that at least one of them had been at the old man's bedside at all times in the remaining months of his life. At no time, claimed the nurses, did Salieri confess to poisoning Mozart. In spite of these statements tending to clear Salieri, many adherents of the poisoning theory continued to suspect him. Perhaps, they suggested, Carpani, the pianist, and the nurses had all lied to cover up for the misdeed of a man they liked and cared about.

The Architects of Murder

In fact, it seems that many people wanted to believe the poisoning theory, whether Salieri or someone else was the guilty party. Other variations of the murder hypothesis emerged over the years, one of the most popular being that a group of conspirators had poisoned Mozart. This view, which began to gain credibility in the 1860s, exploited Mozart's membership in a fraternal organization called the Freemasons. The Freemasons advocated (and, as the Masons, still advocate) brotherhood and moral principles among their members and in society as a whole. For many centuries, however, the organization was very secretive in its meetings, dealings, and initiations. As a result, many people suspected and occasionally accused the Freemasons of dark, sinister, and even antireligious beliefs and deeds. Constanze's sister Sophie encountered this prejudice when she tried to find a priest to administer the last rites of the church to her dying brother-in-law. Several priests refused to attend the composer on the grounds that he was a Freemason.

The most extreme opponents of Freemasonry in the 1700s and 1800s claimed that the organization was one of several secret societies controlled by a single and very evil group. Scholar William Stafford sums up this view in his book *The Mozart Myths:*

In this depiction of an eighteenth-century Freemason lodge meeting, a new member is being ceremoniously inducted into the fraternal organization.

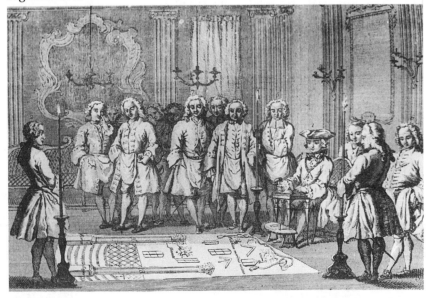

For thousands of years a secret conspiratorial organization [supposedly] has been active in the world; it became especially vigorous in the eighteenth century. . . . Its aims are world domination, free love, and the worship of nature. It masquerades behind the ideals of freedom and equality, but in truth seeks a new order of power and domination; it has a low view of the common people and of women, wishing to reduce them to a degraded and bestial condition. It is ready to use violent means to attain its ends. It fears only one enemy, namely Christianity.

Supposedly, after Mozart joined the Freemasons, he learned about the secret group of men that controlled it, and their beliefs and aims appalled him. He refused to cooperate with them, it is said, and they ordered him killed. According to this theory, the clarinettist Anton Stadler, himself a Freemason, administered the poison over the course of several weeks, having gained repeated entrance to the composer's apartment to check on the progress of the Clarinet Concerto. The commission of the concerto itself was said to have been part of the murder plan. The architects of the murder then ordered that Mozart be "buried like a dog" in a pauper's grave to help erase his memory and as a mark of disrespect.

The seal of the Vienna Masonic lodge to which Mozart belonged.

The main problem with this conspiracy theory, which remained popular in some European circles well into the twentieth century, is that not a shred of convincing evidence exists to support any part of it. Historians and scholars have been unable to uncover any compelling proof for the existence of an ancient and secret organization trying to dominate the world. And there is no evidence whatever implicating Stadler or any of Mozart's other Freemason brothers in the composer's death.

Furthermore, contrary to the romantic account, Mozart was not buried in a pauper's grave. Local burial records show that he received a regular "third-class" funeral, which was then common for Germans of limited financial means. According to the custom of the time, five or six coffins were stacked in a single burial plot to save space in cemeteries; headstones were not permitted. After nine years the coffins were removed, to make way for new ones, and either burned or reburied in obscure locations. It was not unusual, therefore, for the remains of people dead for a decade or more to be destroyed or lost, with no record of the final resting place.

In the Absence of Proof

The secret patron, Antonio Salieri, and the Freemasons are not the only suspects rumored to have poisoned Mozart. Perhaps the most unusual theory in this regard suggests that the composer unwittingly poisoned himself. According to this view, he caught syphilis, a serious sexually transmitted disease, and undertook on his own a common treatment of the time—swallowing mercury chloride. Accidental overdoses of mercury, a highly toxic metal, then slowly but steadily killed him.

Though logical and fascinating, this scenario of self-inflicted poisoning, like the conspiracy hypothesis, suffers from lack of proof. No evidence exists in Mozart's letters or those of his family and friends, or in his doctor's records, that the composer had syphilis. And it is extremely unlikely that Dr. Closset, in his several examinations of the deathly ill man, would have failed to notice the telltale signs of mercury poisoning, not to mention syphilis. Closset himself had published a medical article in 1783, only eight years before Mozart's death, in which he clearly described the cloudy urine, foul breath, and rank-smelling sweat of mercury overdose victims.

Indeed, the very fact that examinations of Mozart by a physician did not reveal any signs of poisoning is the strongest piece of evidence against the theory. To be sure that poisons were not involved, in fact, Dr. Closset consulted with a colleague, Mathias von Sallaba, an expert on poisons and their effects. The two physicians ruled out not only mercury but also acqua toffana, a poison suggested by some theorists. The composer evidently displayed none of the easily detectable symptoms produced by arsenic, the most lethal ingredient of acqua toffana.

Might Mozart have died from the effects of a poison with which the medical authorities of his day were unfamiliar? Certainly, this

Mozart's tragic and mysterious death inspired many later paintings and statues, including this 1877 French sculpture, titled "Death of Mozart."

cannot be ruled out. But in the absence of any sort of proof of such an allegation, it makes sense to examine other theories for which some evidence *does* exist. These theories describe problems ranging from disease and head injuries to exhaustion and clinical depression.

3 *The Medical Detectives: Did Mozart Die of Disease?*

In the twentieth century, many scholars rejected the most popular and romantic version of Mozart's death—namely, the idea that he was poisoned. They focused instead on his chronically poor physical condition, which was both caused and complicated throughout his life by the occurrence of many serious illnesses. The researchers pointed out that Mozart was a frail man whose repeated bouts with disease very likely caused him to become increasingly unhealthy as he grew older. Thus weakened, he became more and more susceptible to more and various ailments, which in turn inflicted additional damage. Eventually, according to this "disease theory," the composer's body could not absorb further punishment and one or more of the ailments proved fatal.

On the surface, the idea that Mozart died of disease seems straightforward and easily provable. After all, Dr. Closset examined him and recorded his symptoms, including fever, rash, and swelling of the hands and feet. These symptoms are consistent with disease, especially since poisoning had been ruled out by Dr. Closset. However, the determination of exactly which disease killed the composer is complicated by a number of factors. First, his symptoms could have been produced by many different ailments. Second, we have only a small number of eyewitness accounts testifying to his physical condition in his last days of life. Except for Dr. Closset, all the witnesses were laypersons with limited medical knowledge. Constanze, Sophie, Süssmayer, and the others could easily have overlooked subtle symptoms, or misunderstood or misinterpreted those they did see.

Moreover, in retrospect, even Dr. Closset was not a highly reliable witness. His observations and diagnosis must be viewed in the context of the age in which he lived—and medical science in the late eighteenth century was primitive compared with present-day

Mozart plays for a small audience of admirers. Despite frequent illnesses, he performed often.

knowledge. This Austrian physician, like all his colleagues, was simply unfamiliar with many diseases and the conditions that caused them. Indeed, the discovery of the germ theory of disease was still decades away, and Dr. Closset had little understanding of the causes of most of the illnesses he *was* familiar with.

For these reasons, modern adherents of the disease theory had to become, in a way, medical detectives. They had to collect, sift through, and examine a small number of clues, some of them vague and confusing, and from this paltry evidence construct a believable theory. Considering that this evidence can be interpreted in so many different ways, it is not surprising that researchers have suggested various diseases and complications to explain Mozart's death.

A Continuous Battle with Disease

All the disease detectives began in the same place—the composer's childhood, for they knew that Mozart was sick on and off throughout his short life. Whatever illness eventually killed him, researchers reasoned, might have been related to one or more that had struck him in the past. Luckily, a fairly reliable catalog of the composer's childhood diseases exists. This is because his father, Leopold Mozart, who was a careful observer and reporter, wrote long letters to family members describing each of his young son's illnesses. The adult Mozart was far less methodical, however; he did not bother to write down the details of many of his sicknesses, and those he did record were not very precise. Thus, his medical record for the last fifteen years of his life is spotty and open to considerable debate and interpretation.

According to the available evidence, Mozart's first serious encounter with illness occurred at age six, when he suffered from an

Leopold Mozart, a fine musician and composer in his own right, wrote a number of letters to relatives describing his son's illnesses.

infection of his upper respiratory tract, that is, the nasal passages and the throat. At the time, doctors did not know that many such infections were caused by streptococci, microscopic bacteria that can multiply in the mucous membranes, the soft, warm, moist tissues of the respiratory system. From Leopold Mozart's detailed descriptions, the consensus of modern medical researchers is that the boy's infection was streptococcal. Young Mozart endured two painful relapses of the infection in 1762.

In that same year he also contracted a mild case of rheumatic fever, which was likely a by-product of his strep infections. According to William Stafford:

> Even today the mechanism of [physical process involved in] rheumatic fever is not perfectly understood. It is a secondary illness, occurring two or more weeks after the primary infection, commonly of the upper air passages . . . by streptococci (chain-form bacteria). It produces fever with much sweating and attacks tissues of a certain kind, initially in the joints, especially of the hands, knees, and feet. These become swollen, inflamed and terribly painful—so painful that the patient cannot bear to be touched or to have the joints covered. The agony makes it impossible to move. In spite of the pain, the affliction of the joints is neither lasting nor dangerous. The danger of the illness derives from the fact that in the majority of cases it also attacks the heart, causing permanent damage to the valves, especially when it recurs.

Mozart, age 4

Two years later, in 1764, Mozart suffered from another respiratory problem, tonsillitis, an inflammation of the tonsils, which are tissue masses in the back of the throat. And the following year he came down with typhoid fever, a very infectious bacterial disease spread via contaminated food and water. The symptoms he exhibited, as recorded by his father, were classic for the disease: a slow pulse, weight loss, skin rash, high fever, bleed-

Illness in Vienna

In this September 14, 1784, letter to his daughter, (excerpted from The Letters of Mozart and His Family, *edited by Emily Anderson), Leopold Mozart described Wolfgang's current illness, the identity of which has become a matter of debate among modern scholars.*

"My son has been very ill in Vienna. At a performance of [Italian composer Giovanni] Paisiello's new opera [*Il Re Teodoro in Venezia*, performed on August 23, 1784] he perspired so profusely that his clothes were drenched and in the cold night air he had to try to find his servant who had his overcoat, as in the meantime an order had been given that no servant was to be allowed into the theater by the ordinary entrance [so that wealthy patrons would not have to mingle with servants]. So not only my son, but a number of people caught rheumatic fever, which became septic [rotten or poisonous] when not taken in hand [treated] at once. My son writes as follows: 'Four days running at the very same hour I had a fearful attack of colic [severe abdominal pain], which ended each time in violent vomiting. I have therefore to be extremely careful. My doctor is Sigmund Barisani, who since his arrival in Vienna has been almost daily at my rooms. People here praise him very highly. He is very clever too and you will find that in a short time he will make his way [become successful and well-known].'"

ing from the mucous membranes, and pneumonia. The boy also lapsed into a coma for a short time.

These early illnesses marked only the beginning of Mozart's continuous battle with disease. Among the ailments he endured in the next twenty-three years were the following: in 1766, a second attack of rheumatic fever; in 1767, smallpox, a highly infectious disease characterized by high fever and skin sores; in 1770, severe frostbite; in 1771, hepatitis, an inflammation of the liver; in 1774, a severe dental abscess, or infection in the mouth; in 1780, bronchitis, an inflammation of the mucous membranes in the bronchi, the tubes leading into the lungs; in 1784, a third siege of rheumatic fever; and in 1787, another serious streptococcal infection.

An Excess of Bile

Mozart's extensive medical record of debilitating conditions became the basis for the disease theory of his death. After examining the record and correlating it with the known symptoms of his final illness, several scholars concluded that the composer died of complications of earlier chronic conditions. A few such conclusions appeared in print in the 1800s and early 1900s. But because of the widespread popularity of the poisoning theory, these suppositions did not cause much of a stir. A number of more thorough studies of the disease hypothesis, researches that benefited from modern advances in medical knowledge, appeared in the 1960s, 1970s, and 1980s. The results fell into two broad categories. The first suggested that Mozart's final illness was brought on by a new attack of rheumatic fever. The second cited kidney failure due to complications from repeated streptococcal infections as the agent of death.

Two pieces of evidence seem to lend support to the rheumatic fever thesis. The first is Mozart's symptoms, especially his elevated temperature and swollen hands and feet, which are consistent with the disease. Skin rashes are much rarer in cases of rheumatic fever. But the generally dirty and unsanitary conditions common in the eighteenth century, combined with the composer's profuse sweating, could have accounted for the rash mentioned by Dr. Closset.

The second bit of evidence in favor of rheumatic fever is the composer's lengthy history of experience with the illness. Usually, each successive attack, particularly a severe one, damages the heart; which grows weaker and weaker. As far as is known, Mozart did not exhibit any signs of a weak heart. Nevertheless, as Stafford points out, "damaged heart valves may produce no symptoms for many years, until suddenly some exertion, or infection, brings on a heart attack." Thus, a new outbreak of rheumatic fever may have delivered a final blow to the composer's heart. If so, Dr. Closset might have missed a diagnosis of heart failure partly because he hadn't looked for it; not only had he assumed his patient's heart was strong, but he was concentrating on the fever.

In fact, a document from the era following Mozart's death supports both the rheumatic fever thesis and the idea that Dr. Closset grossly misdiagnosed the specific cause of death. In addition to the poison expert, Dr. Sallaba, Dr. Closset consulted with other colleagues about Mozart's deteriorating condition. One of these was Guldener von Lobes, the medical supervisor for the German region known as Lower Austria, who in 1824 recalled:

> [Mozart] fell sick in the late autumn [of 1791] of a rheumatic and inflammatory fever, which, being fairly general among us at the time, attacked many people. I did not know about it until a few days later, when his condition had already grown much worse. I did not visit him for some reason, but informed myself of his condition through Dr. Closset, with whom I came in contact almost every day. The latter considered Mozart's illness to be dangerous, and from the very beginning feared a fatal conclusion, namely a deposit on the brain. One day he met Dr. Sallaba and he said positively, "Mozart is lost, it is no longer

One of the many portraits of Mozart produced years after his death.

possible to restrain the deposit." Sallaba communicated this information to me at once, and in fact Mozart died a few days later with the usual symptoms of a deposit on the brain.

By claiming that the immediate cause of Mozart's death was a "deposit on the brain," the doctors betrayed their own ignorance and the elementary state of the medical science of the day. Because they did not yet know about germs, doctors attributed disease to other causes, most of which were later proven incorrect. Thomas Closset and his colleagues thought that rheumatic fever and several other diseases resulted from an imbalance of a deadly substance known as "black bile." Supposedly, a *materia morbifica*, or excess amount, of this thick liquid in the body made a person sick. In severe cases this excess was believed to travel to the head, where it lodged as a "deposit on the brain," almost always a fatal development.

Belief in this imaginary excess of bile may explain the vagueness of Dr. Closset's official declaration of the cause of death. Dr. von Lobes specifically named Mozart's condition "a rheumatic and inflammatory fever," and since he himself did not examine the patient, he must have received the information from Dr. Closset. This raises the question of why Dr. Closset listed the illness as a "fever," as opposed to the narrower designation "rheumatic fever." In the absence of documentary evidence, it is impossible to say for certain. But given the prevailing wisdom that fevers from various ailments could cause an excess of bile to migrate to the brain, Dr. Closset may have felt that the more general term "fever" was sufficient for his death report. The attending physician also failed to mention any "deposit on the brain." In those days, however, educated people believed that fevers severe enough to cause death always were accompanied by such a bilious deposit. Given the strength of this connection, Dr. Closset may have failed to mention a deposit because he expected that anyone who read the death report would automatically assume that one had been present.

Kidneys and Colic
The evidence for the other medical theory extensively researched in the 1960s and 1970s, kidney failure, is far less convincing. The most influential proponent of the theory was Aloys Greither, a Ger-

man doctor who advocated it in a series of articles spanning almost two decades. According to Greither, each of the composer's bouts of streptococcal infection caused an inflammation of his kidneys, which, in turn, led to cirrhosis, or permanent scarring, of those organs. Supposedly, during Mozart's final illness, his kidneys began to give out. They were unable to separate urine from blood, with the result that the body retained fluid, swelling noticeably. The retention of urine, a waste product, eventually caused him to go into a coma and die.

This hypothesis relies on the idea that Mozart suffered from chronic kidney problems for most of his adult life. But is there any evidence that this was true? Greither and his supporters point to an excerpt from a letter written in 1784 by Leopold Mozart to his daughter Nannerl:

> My son has been very ill in Vienna. At a performance of [Italian composer Giovanni] Paisiello's new opera he perspired so profusely that his clothes were drenched and in the cold night air he had to try to find his servant who had his overcoat. . . . Wolfgang writes as follows: "Four days running at the very same hour I had a violent attack of colic [severe abdominal pain], which ended each time in violent vomiting. I have therefore to be extremely careful."

Because severe inflammation of the kidneys can produce heavy sweating, abdominal pain, and vomiting, the letter might indeed suggest that Mozart suffered from recurring kidney problems, or at least that he had one bad attack.

Conclusions Unlikely

However, critics of this idea say that the references in the letter are far too sketchy and uncertain to make such a diagnosis. For one thing, they point out, later in the letter Leopold Mozart mentioned that a large number of Viennese were sick at the same time as his son and with the same illness, which he described as rheumatic fever. It is extremely unlikely that many people in one city would be reported as suffering simultaneously from kidney disease, which at that time was far less often diagnosed than rheumatic fever.

Moreover, say critics, the same symptoms described in the letter can be attributed to other ailments. Among these is gastroenteritis,

A woodcut depicts a doctor bleeding a patient.

an inflammation of the intestines, which, like rheumatic fever, was much more common than kidney disease in Mozart's time. It is possible that Leopold Mozart's mention of rheumatic fever was based on mistaken rumors or misdiagnoses by local doctors. In that case, his son, along with many other Viennese, could well have been suffering from gastroenteritis, perhaps brought on by food poisoning. Before the advent of the germ theory made people careful and before the need to refrigerate perishable dishes was recognized, spoiled meat and other contaminated foods frequently initiated outbreaks of food poisoning. A clue that supports this scenario is the elder Mozart's use of the German word for "septic" to describe the illness in question. In the eighteenth century, that term was often applied to rotten or poisonous substances.

Another weakness of the kidney failure theory is that massive urine retention causes a general swelling of most of the patient's body. Yet both Constanze and her sister Sophie clearly described Mozart's swelling as being confined to his limbs, particularly the hands and feet. This kind of swelling is more consistent with diseases such as rheumatic fever.

Blood in a Pan

Thus, a comparison of the rheumatic fever and kidney failure theories seems to favor the former. But even if Mozart did have rheumatic fever, it is entirely possible that a complication of the disease, rather than the disease itself, did him in. In the last thirty years, some researchers, including Swiss dentist and medical writer Carl Bär, have proposed that Dr. Closset inadvertently killed his famous patient. In the 1700s, doctors routinely practiced venesection, or "bleeding." In this procedure, a doctor opened a patient's vein and allowed varying amounts of blood to flow out into a pan. While bleeding was thought to be good for a wide variety of conditions, it was used in cases of rheumatic fever because it supposedly relieved the buildup of excess black bile.

Both Sophie and another eyewitness stated that Mozart was bled several times. "Even a conservative estimate indicates that Mozart in all probability lost roughly two liters [about 4.2 pints] of blood," wrote Dr. Bär. It is at least possible, therefore, that the composer's loss of blood weakened his system and injured his heart, already impaired by three bouts of rheumatic fever.

Of course because modern researchers can make only educated guesses about the extent of Mozart's blood loss, there is no way to be sure that this is what killed him. Similarly, the rheumatic fever and kidney failure theories are based only on fragmentary, centuries-old evidence, most of it clearly open to interpretation. Like so many other theories concerning Mozart's strange death, they remain intriguing but uncertain.

4 Between Body and Soul: Did Exhaustion Destroy Mozart?

No scholar or historian doubts that Mozart was extremely ill in his last few weeks of life and that this illness contributed to his death. However, some researchers have suggested that additional factors were at work, elements of his life and personality that caused his ailments to become more frequent and more severe. Of these factors, one of the most often cited is physical and mental exhaustion. According to this view, by cramming more work and play into each year than an average person did in ten, Mozart almost literally burned himself out. Unable to withstand the constant strain, his frail body succumbed to bouts of illness that he otherwise might have survived.

Mozart conducts in the cathedral of Salzburg, in his time an independent principality. The city was not incorporated into Austria until 1816.

To support this view, many biographers and others who have written about the composer have emphasized what they describe as his unusual lifestyle and mental outlook. Mozart was, they say, an immature adult, a child who never grew up. From a physical standpoint, as an adult he displayed childlike energy levels and drove himself at an incredible and exhausting pace. And like a spoiled child, he was extravagant, irresponsible with money, and always ready to indulge in any whim that suited his fancy. As a result, he was a social misfit. Often, he was temperamental and tactless, showing a coarse and obscene sense of humor that offended people. Recognizing these faults, but unable to control or to eliminate them, he developed feelings of inadequacy that made him strive harder and harder to make people like and respect him. The only effective way he knew of gaining that respect was by writing music, and he threw himself into his work with a vengeance. In short, too fast-paced a life, coupled with constant overwork and frequent sickness, exhausted and killed him. "No need for poison here," wrote Ignaz Arnold, an early Mozart biographer, "nor for a secret messenger . . . nor for a *Requiem*—his powers were worn out, his constitution destroyed."

An Amazing Output

Arnold was perhaps the first author strongly to emphasize the theme of exhaustion in Mozart's life and to implicate that theme in the composer's death. Arnold wrote:

> What straining of his imagination, what constant wearing-down of his spirit, what excitement of his brain fibers! What continuous sapping of his vital forces! In a word: his whole life was—the consumption of life. History shows us a host of great spirits who burned themselves out.

Here, the biographer was referring to the exhaustion of Mozart's "creative energies," a process that is probably imaginary. In the realms of art, music, and literature, the nineteenth century was a highly romantic age. Many people were fascinated with great artists and other geniuses and how their minds worked. Arnold's mention of "sapping the vital forces" reflects a common but flawed assumption of his day, namely, that a great artist's imagination and other creative gifts could be drained away, exhausted, or even destroyed by overuse. Supposedly the production of a masterpiece strained and weakened an artist's creative energies more than the generation of a lesser work. Hence, by this reasoning, Mozart created masterpiece after masterpiece, and eventually exhausted his talent.

To his credit, Arnold also discussed the composer's *physical* exhaustion, brought on by sheer overwork as well as by a host of other activities. Later writers, even those who supported other theories for Mozart's death, could not help but find the composer's average physical output amazing. As an example of this output, Braunbehrens summarizes Mozart's creations and major activities for a single year—1784:

Six piano concertos [works for piano and full orchestra], one piano quintet [for piano and four wind instruments], one string quartet, and two sonatas [works for one or two instruments having three or four movements each] and two sets of variations for piano are listed [in the catalog of his works], as well as a few smaller compositions. This enormous output was not the work of a composer writing in undisturbed peace and seclusion, but of one whose schedule included teaching obligations, subscription concerts, private concerts, houseguests, and two changes of residence, as well as all kinds of other distractions, any one of which would have been enough to make an ordinary person nervous. Altogether, twenty-six concert appearances are recorded for that year. . . . [His] creative phases were so intense that they must have been an excessive strain on his [physical] energies.

This tremendous and continuous physical output was all the more amazing considering that Mozart was small, frail, and lacking in bodily strength and endurance. All the surviving physical descriptions of the composer match that of German scholar and

Mozart plays the spinet, an early version of the harpsichord, in about 1786. This rendering accurately depicts the composer as thin and frail.

teacher Friedrich Schlichtegroll, who wrote in 1793, less than two years after Mozart's death, "Mozart was not distinguished by an especially striking physical appearance. . . . He was small, thin, pale, and his features betrayed nothing out of the ordinary." According to other accounts, the composer was short (apparently about five foot three or four inches) and of "very slight build."

Despite his delicate frame, which became progressively weaker under the nearly constant onslaught of illness, Mozart almost never slowed his pace. Year after year, often while sick, he continued to compose, to give and attend concerts, to travel, to teach, and to rush from one appointment to the next. Even when sitting down, he could not keep still. According to Schlichtegroll, "His body was in constant motion; he always had to be doing something with his hands or feet. . . . Even his face did not stay constant."

Always a Child

Given these descriptions of the composer, some writers have suggested that his extraordinary spirit was, in a sense, at war with his less than ordinary body. His desire to create and accomplish was overpowering. But his physical constitution was not up to the task. And it was as though, in his frustration over this inequity, he pushed himself relentlessly, testing and often exceeding his physical limits. In his 1945 biographical study entitled *Mozart: His Character, His Work*, writer Alfred Einstein summarized this portrait of a man locked in battle with himself:

> There is a strange kind of human being in whom there is an eternal struggle between body and soul, animal and god, for dominance. In all great men [and women] this mixture is striking, and in none more so than in Wolfgang Amadeus Mozart.

But was frustration over physical inadequacies the only factor that drove Mozart constantly to test his bodily limits and finally, and fatally, to exhaust himself? A number of biographers and researchers have suggested that he felt inadequate in other ways, too. For instance, a substantial amount of evidence suggests that he was socially maladjusted. In other words, he was unable and/or unwilling to adhere or adjust to many of the accepted, sensible, and polite social customs of the day. According to this view, as a result he tended to feel apart from and rejected by many members of the European upper classes, among whom both he and his father had hoped he would come to live. In his frustration, the younger Mozart sought acceptance through his music. And in his desire to please, he overworked himself.

Part of the evidence regularly cited to support this viewpoint comes from contemporary sources that describe Mozart as never having grown up. Typical is the postscript to a letter from Nannerl Mozart to Schlichtegroll in 1792, which states, "Apart from his music he was almost always a child, and thus he remained: and this is a main feature of his character on the dark side; he always needed a father's, a mother's or some guardian's care."

One apparent proof of the composer's immaturity was his inability to manage his own financial affairs. As Michael Parouty puts it:

> It is clear that he had no idea how to handle money—he tried for a short while to keep track of his [bank] accounts and to catalogue his [musical] works, but neither effort lasted. Constanze [out of her great love for him] was content to live from hand to mouth, spending money when there was any and concentrating on keeping up appearances [so that people would not see how poor they were and look down on them]. She was almost continually pregnant, and

This letter from Mozart to friend Johann Michael Puchberg contains a desperate appeal for money. Puchberg, a rich merchant and fellow Mason, often loaned the debt-ridden composer the funds he needed to keep going.

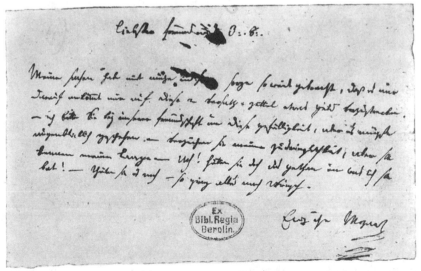

the two went from illness to illness, barely keeping their heads above water.

Amply supporting this scenario are frequent phrases in Leopold Mozart's letters, such as: "Do you think that Wolfgang will now attend to his affairs? I hope he has got accustomed to doing this and that his head is not always full of music."

In addition, Mozart consistently lived above his means. He had a passion for buying fine clothes and at various times he kept a horse and even six ponies, which required expensive upkeep. He also had a billiard table, his own carriage, and other expensive items, and he threw lavish parties. Some of this high lifestyle may have been designed to impress the nobles and gain entrance into their social circles. But he never had much acceptance in these groups. And he kept on borrowing money from friends and spending it foolishly until he was hopelessly in debt.

The Crudest Possible Humor

Evidently, Mozart's lack of maturity often caused him to behave in ways that offended people, especially the "well-bred" members of the upper classes, the very people who most often commissioned his music. Both verbally and in writing, he frequently used the crudest possible bathroom humor and foul language. For example, in 1777, when he was twenty-one, he wrote to his cousin Maria Anna Thekla Mozart:

> Oh, my arse [rear end] is burning like fire! What on earth does it mean?—Perhaps some fart wants to come out? Why yes, fart, I know, see and smell you . . . and . . . what is that?—Is it possible . . . Ye gods! Can I believe those ears of mine? Yes indeed, it is so—what a long melancholy [sad] note [musical sound]!

In that same year, the composer recited rude limericks containing obscene words and references in front of a group of court musicians. And he even gave some of his most famous musical works smutty titles, apparently attempting some kind of shock value. For example, two of his canons, or songs in the "round" style, bear the titles *"Leck mich im Arsch"* ["Lick my Arse"] and *"Leck mir den Arsch fein recht schön sauber"* ["Lick my Arse Until It's Nice and Clean"].

Some writers have tried to excuse Mozart's bad taste, arguing that his vulgarities were not unusual for the day. According to this view,

"The Princess Dunghill"

Among the many examples of Mozart's profanity, bathroom humor, and vulgar insults is this excerpt from another 1777 letter to his father, Leopold (quoted in The Letters of Mozart and His Family*). Mozart held many members of the aristocracy in contempt, as evidenced from this humorous but biting description of some of the nobles he had encountered at a concert.*

"A great crowd of nobility was there: the Duchess Smackbottom, the Countess Makewater [urinate], to say nothing of the Princess Dunghill with her two daughters, who, however, are already married to the two princes Potbelly von Pigtail."

many people then regularly swore and told dirty jokes, just as they do today. However, even today, in a much more permissive age, such behavior is usually considered unacceptable in public and at polite social functions. There is little doubt that the composer's off-color language and humor often offended and alienated people.

Lending further support to the idea that Mozart was immature and socially maladjusted is evidence that he had scandalous sexual affairs with women, regardless of the possible damage to his marriage and reputation. He was rumored to have slept with several of his female piano students. Indeed, the husband of one of these pupils was so angered that on the day after Mozart's death he wounded his wife with a knife and then cut his own throat. Supposedly, the composer also had affairs with opera singers he met while working in and attending the theater, and even with his cousin Maria. Although many of these relationships cannot be absolutely confirmed, certain notes and letters he wrote to women, unbeknownst to Constanze, do support the suspicion that he cheated on her. For example, in an October 1782 letter to an aristocratic lady, a baroness he had met at a Viennese ball, he wrote:

Since the night I saw your ladyship at the ball with your hair so beautifully dressed—gone is my peace of mind! . . . You smile! You blush! Ah, yes—I am indeed happy. My fortune is made! But alas! Who taps me on the shoulder? Who peeps into my letter? Alas! alas! alas! My wife!

Exaggerations and Lies?

What emerges from these accounts is a picture of a man who lived an incredibly fast-paced life, an existence marked by diverse kinds of excess. The combined effects of his grueling sessions of overwork, his irresponsibility, extravagance, alleged womanizing, and his frantic attempts to gain acceptance and respect eventually wore him down. By continuing to weaken a constitution that never was robust, he laid himself wide open to a host of diseases. And from one of these he was too exhausted to recover.

But is this picture completely accurate and believable? That Mozart drove himself unusually hard is certain. And plenty of evidence suggests that he was irresponsible and at least to some degree a social misfit. However, some of the evidence for the composer's supposed excesses may have been exaggerated. As William Stafford suggests, some writers based stories from Mozart's life on earlier versions, which themselves were based on a single and questionable source. And some of the original

"Sheer Garbage"

Another example of Mozart's vulgarity appears in this letter to Leopold, also dated 1777 (quoted in The Letters of Mozart and His Family*). Here, he admits to reciting dirty jokes and poems at a gathering of well-known musicians.*

"I . . . hereby plead guilty and confess that yesterday and the day before (not to mention on several other occasions) I did not get home until midnight; and that from ten o'clock until the said hour . . . in the presence and company of [several respected musicians] . . . I did frequently, without any difficulty, but quite easily, perpetrate [recite]—rhymes, the same being, moreover, sheer garbage, that is, on such subjects as farting, s——tting, and arse-licking. . . . I should not have behaved so godlessly, however, if our ringleader [host] . . . had not egged me on and incited me; at the same time I must admit that I thoroughly enjoyed it. I confess all these sins and transgressions of mine from the bottom of my heart, and in the hope of having to confess them very often I firmly resolve to go on with the sinful life I have begun."

witnesses may have lied. Niemetschek, who himself passed on a number of legends about the composer, admitted, "Mozart's enemies and detractors became so vicious, so outspoken, especially toward his end, and after his death ... this gossiping and lying was so shameless, so scandalous."

Moreover, even if Mozart did exhaust himself to the degree alleged, exhaustion is by no means firmly proven as the principal factor in his death. However much he wore himself down, either poison or disease may still have pushed him over the edge. Or perhaps some other element of his life triggered

Maria Anna Mozart

his destruction. It has been suggested that Mozart's feelings of inadequacy were partly responsible for his driving himself too hard. Could it be that those same feelings also took their toll on his mind? If so, as will be shown, it may have been a kind of mental illness that brought about his untimely death.

5 A Kind of Emptiness: Did Mental Depression Kill Mozart?

Many of the scholars and writers who have studied and written about Mozart, including most who have emphasized the physical exhaustion that overtook the composer in 1791, have commented on his peculiar mental state as an adult. Mozart has been described variously as sad, despondent, miserable, and depressed. Some writers have concluded, therefore, that while sickness and exhaustion surely wore him down, it was mental despair and depression that delivered the deathblow. According to this view, sadness caused him to retreat into his own little, isolated mental world. Eventually, he lost the will to live, and this allowed sickness and exhaustion to destroy him.

Proponents of the idea that Mozart suffered from an extreme and perhaps fatal case of depression have not had to look far for supporting evidence. The composer's adult years were certainly filled with episodes of loss, grief, frustration, and rejection. He lost his mother in 1778 and his father in 1787. The death of his father, with whom he was especially close, left him emotionally devastated, as did the loss of four of his six children. Then there were his professional and financial problems. He was constantly rejected and passed over for important musical positions that would have afforded him the financial security he craved. The unfavorable response to several of his operas by aristocratic Viennese audiences in the 1780s must have been equally disappointing and frustrating. And surely his steady descent into poverty was a source of worry and insecurity.

In addition, almost continual bouts of sickness must have been emotionally as well as physically draining. A sad side effect of chronic illness was the deterioration of Mozart's boyish good looks. As one of his modern biographers, Wolfgang Hildesheimer, comments:

In the last years of his life he became physically unattractive. His face became pockmarked, the skin grew yellowish and puffy; toward the end he developed a double chin [very unusual for a man in his early thirties]. His head was too big for his body. His nose was outsized; a newspaper once called him the "great-nosed Mozart." His eyes protruded more and more; he grew stout [chubby]. He tried always to have a hairstyle which hid the strange malformation [deformity] of his ears [which he had from birth].

Did all these factors combine to throw the composer into a dark mood of despair that eventually killed him?

"A Longing . . . Which Never Ceases"

A case can certainly be made that Mozart experienced repeated and emotionally upsetting professional rejections. As Stafford points out, despite being probably the greatest musical talent of his day, he was a "professional failure in his last years." The Viennese nobility's poor reception of his operas *The Marriage of Figaro* and *Don Giovanni* hurt him deeply. The events following the death in 1790 of Emperor Joseph II, who had shown him a fair amount of generosity in spite of the intrigues of Salieri, were also upsetting for the composer. To his dismay, Mozart found that he was not in favor with either the new emperor, Leopold II, or his imperial court. The first sign of this development was the composer's rejection for the post of assistant kapellmeister for the court. More disturbing still, he was one of the few well-known German musicians not invited to Leopold's coronation in the city of Frankfurt on October 9, 1790. Mozart attended anyway, even though it meant selling some furniture to pay for the trip.

Such repeated professional rejections worsened Mozart's already dire financial situation. To makes ends meet, he was forced to take commissions for musical works to be performed on novelty instruments such as the mechanical organ and the glass harmonica. This was embarrassing for a composer of Mozart's caliber, who increasingly felt that he had failed in his chosen profession.

Feelings of loneliness may also have contributed to Mozart's growing state of mental depression in his final years. His parents had been dead for some time, and he went for long stretches without seeing his sister Nannerl because she and Constanze did not

The 1790 coronation of Leopold II as emperor after the death of his brother, Joseph II, on February 20 of that year. Though not invited, Mozart attended anyway.

get along well. Having been cut off from many professional relationships at court, he also began to withdraw from friends and social acquaintances. In addition, in his last year, 1791, Constanze was almost always either ill or away at the health spa in Baden. Did loneliness take its toll? Describing the depression hypothesis, Stafford writes:

> Mozart could not fail to recognize his professional failure; but the tragedy of his last years was that finally he recognized his social failure also. He realized that he was, and always had been, cut off from others. This knowledge destroyed him, extinguishing his will to live.

One piece of evidence often cited in support of Mozart's deepening depression is an excerpt from his July 7, 1791, letter to his wife, in which he stated:

I can't describe what I have been feeling—a kind of emptiness, which hurts me dreadfully—a kind of longing, which is never satisfied, which never ceases, and which persists, nay rather increases daily. . . . If I go to the piano and sing something out of my opera [*The Magic Flute*, on which he

Playing to the Chairs and Walls

Mozart described one of the most dramatic examples of the poor treatment he received at the hands of European aristocrats in a May 1, 1778, letter to his father. While visiting Paris the young composer received an invitation to play the piano for a noblewoman, the duchess de Chabot. Hoping that it would help him gain a foothold in aristocratic French circles, he gladly accepted the invitation. However, he soon regretted his decision.

"I had to wait for half an hour in a large ice-cold, unheated room, which hadn't even a fireplace. At last the Duchess de Chabot appeared. She was very polite and asked me to make the best of the clavier [keyboard] in the room, as none of her own were in good condition. Would I perhaps try it? I said that I would be delighted to play something, but that it was impossible at the moment, as my fingers were numb with cold; and I asked her to have me taken at least to a room where there was a fire. 'Oh yes, sir, you are right,' was all the reply I got. She then sat down and began to draw and continued to do so for a whole hour, having as company some gentlemen, who all sat in a circle round a big table, while I had the honor to wait. The windows and doors were open and not only my hands but my whole body and my feet were frozen and my head began to ache. . . . At last, to cut my story short, I played on that miserable, wretched pianoforte instrument. But what vexed me most of all was that Madame and all her gentlemen never interrupted their drawing for a moment, but went on intently, so that I had to play to the chairs, tables and walls."

was then working], I have to stop at once, for this stirs my emotions too deeply.

Various writers have also pointed out passages in Mozart's music that seem to reflect an increasingly sad, dark, and gloomy emotional state. For instance, the biographer Einstein refers to "demonic" elements, as well as "dark eruptions" and an "explosion of dark, tragic, passionate emotions," in the composer's Piano Concerto in C Minor (written in 1786). Hildesheimer hears a "gloomy agitation" in the same piece. And Braunbehrens calls attention to the words from an aria, or song, from the opera *Idomeneo*. "Fear not, my love," wails the character Idamante, "my heart beats always for you. Cruel, merciless stars, have you no pity? Lovely souls, you who see how I am suffering now, tell me if a faithful heart can stand such misery."

Tuning Out the Real World

Another claim often made about Mozart's mental/emotional state in his last years is that he became increasingly isolated. According to a number of contemporary witnesses, the composer regularly

Mozart with Nannerl, his father Leopold, and a portrait of Leopold's wife, Anna Maria, in 1781.

and suddenly "tuned out" the sounds and stimuli of the real world and retreated into the mysterious realm of his own mind. This, they implied, was a long-held habit that became more pronounced in his final years. One such witness was Joseph Lange, Mozart's brother-in-law, who painted a famous unfinished portrait of the composer. After Mozart's death, Lange wrote:

> Never was Mozart less recognizably a great man in his conversations and actions, than when he was busied with an important work. At such times he not only spoke confusedly and disconnectedly, but . . . even deliberately forgot himself in his behavior. But he did not appear to be brooding and thinking about anything.

Even more revealing was the testimony of Mozart's sister-in-law Sophie, who recalled in 1828:

> Even in his best mood . . . at the same time looking one straight in the eye, giving a deliberate answer to any question . . . he seemed at the same time to be working away deep in thought at something quite different. Even when he washed his hands in the early morning, he walked up and down the room at the same time, never standing still, at the same time tapped one heel against the other and was always thoughtful. At table [meals] he often took a corner of his napkin, crumpled it up lightly, rubbed it round below his nose, and appeared in his thoughtfulness to be unaware of what he was doing.

Was such behavior a sign of some kind of mental illness? There is little doubt that Mozart became increasingly irritable and unstable in his last few years. Perhaps his tendency regularly to isolate himself mentally from the rest of the world paralleled his growing physical isolation from family and friends. If so, retreating into his mind may have been a way of escaping his increasingly unhappy life. It may also have been a symptom of a deepening and dangerous mental depression. "It is possible," remarks Hildesheimer, "that there was some reciprocity [direct relationship] between his [odd] conduct and his growing isolation [from people and society], that he reacted morbidly [in an unhealthy way] to his isolation and his reaction deepened it." Thus, the weirder he acted, the more uncomfortable he made his friends, and the more they avoided him.

Toward the end, even Constanze, who loved him passionately, often felt that he was ignoring her.

A Dark View of Genius

Assuming for the moment that Mozart was indeed a mentally unstable man in his later years, the question arises: What made him that way? A response suggesting grief, frustration, rejection, and chronic sickness may not tell the whole story. Many people suffer from some or even all of these problems and manage to function fairly normally. And some of the most commonly cited evidence for the composer's depression can be interpreted in other ways. For example, the "emptiness" and "ceaseless longing" he mentioned in his letter to Constanze might well have been expressions of his missing her, rather than of being depressed. "You cannot imagine how I have been aching for you all this while," he wrote in the same letter.

Not surprisingly, several scholars have tried to provide more extreme and more exotic explanations for Mozart's depression and instability. The most popular of these explanations in the nineteenth century centered around the "tragic genius" cliché. In the literature and arts of that highly romantic age, this meant a person who displayed not only intellectual superiority, but also emotional instability and bizarre, even antisocial behavior. As Stafford explains:

> Genius understood in this way is supernatural. It puts the person it possesses in touch with a mysterious and hidden realm lying beneath or behind commonplace surface appearances. Romanticism has a dark side, reflected in its interest in the "gothic," the unearthly and even the satanic; a dark view of genius sees it as a demonic force which speaks through the artist. . . . [This concept] proposes that genius is divorced from the ordinary world, passionate, sensual, rebellious, disruptive, childlike. It makes possible the image of a strangely divided being, an insignificant mortal who is merely the medium through which inspiration speaks.

According to this view, Mozart could not help being mentally ill. As an inevitable facet of his personality, his genius doomed him to a miserable life and a premature death.

The famous portrait painted in 1789–1790 by Joseph Lange, Constanze's brother-in-law.

But this concept may have more to do with the romantic visions of nineteenth-century writers than with the realities of Mozart's life. Some evidence exists that he had a high opinion of his talents: A few phrases in Leopold Mozart's letters state, in effect, "You may think of yourself as a genius, but . . ." Almost certainly, however, Mozart's concept of genius was different from that of the later romanticists. In musical terms, he likely saw a genius as one who was superior to others in craftsmanship, that is, the ability to devise pleasing melodies and orchestrate them inventively. That many aristocrats did not recognize the magnitude of his accomplishments undoubtedly angered and frustrated him. But none of the unflattering references to members of the nobility in his letters suggests that this caused him agonizing depression.

Rebel with a Cause

Another theory suggests that Mozart's mental instability was the result of his being an artistic rebel. According to this view, the art patrons and upper-class socialites of his day received much of his music coolly and sometimes even rejected it because it was too sophisticated for their tastes. He could have written the kind of music they wanted and enjoyed success. But for him music was more than a profession and a passion. It was a cause to fight for. To take an artistic stand and also to show his contempt for those who had rejected him, he refused to change his composing style, regardless of the consequences. These consequences turned out to be continued exclusion of him from the social circles of the nobility, poverty, overwork, and death.

This theory has a number of problems—not least that many members of the Austrian nobility admired a large proportion of Mozart's musical works. It was his operas, mainly some of his later and highly inventive ones, that were coolly received. Moreover, it was primarily Viennese audiences, which did tend to be musically unsophisticated, that rejected the operas. Audiences in a number of other European cities embraced these works. Also, as

In Mozart's day, many European cities had elegant opera houses like this one. At one time or another while he was still living, nearly all featured performances of the composer's works.

Stafford and others have pointed out, Mozart's contempt for and stubborness in dealing with the nobility may not have been the result of conscious rebellion against a specific group. He may have been a proud artist who refused to lower his musical standards for anyone.

The concept of Mozart as a depressed, lonely, rebellious, and tragic genius is both dramatic and romantic. But it is this very combination of drama and romanticism that makes the idea suspect. By the early twentieth century, the romantic vision of the tragic genius had lost much of its credibility and acceptance. Therefore, most modern scholars classify the concept of mental depression extinguishing Mozart's will to live as a colorful exaggeration of what were essentially normal periods of sadness, grief, frustration, and disappointment. For a more believable explanation for his death, they say, it is necessary to search elsewhere.

6 Will the Mystery of Mozart's Death Ever Be Solved?

The search goes on for the cause or causes of the mysterious death of Wolfgang Amadeus Mozart. This does not mean that some of the older theories—for example, those implicating rheumatic fever, exhaustion, or depression—are wrong. Each of these explanations, however, lacks enough undeniable, unshakable evidence to make it conclusive. And thus researchers keep on looking.

The newest studies of Mozart's demise always have one important advantage over prior ones. This is the expansion and improvement of historical and scientific knowledge, as well as investigative tools and techniques. In particular, medical knowledge and technology undergo impressive advances with each passing year. New studies, aided by rapidly improving computer technology, allow doctors to describe previously unknown medical conditions and to better understand familiar ones. It is not surprising, therefore, that the latest and perhaps most intriguing speculations about Mozart's death are medical.

A Blood Clot on the Heart

One of the newest theories was proposed by Willem Boissevain in 1990. This German scholar suggests that the composer died of infective, or bacterial, endocarditis, a serious type of heart disease unknown to doctors before the twentieth century. Endocarditis consists of a bacteria-infected blood clot that grows directly on one of the heart valves. As the heart pumps away, the infection spreads, via the bloodstream, throughout the body. At the same time, the infected valve undergoes progressive damage, grows weaker, and can sometimes even perforate, or rupture, an event that can, in turn, lead to heart failure.

Endocarditis develops in a way that does correspond with certain aspects of Mozart's peculiar medical history. First, like rheumatic fever, the disease is a secondary illness that develops after an infection elsewhere in the body. Endocarditis can be triggered by streptococcal infections, by tonsillitis, or by infections acquired during extensive dental work. As discussed earlier, Mozart had numerous strep infections, as well as tonsillitis and gum infections requiring dental work. Endocarditis can also be caused by the taking of blood in unsanitary conditions. Dr. Closset bled the composer perhaps two or more times and, since people were unaware of the existence of germs, it is quite unlikely that these procedures were performed under sterile conditions. Thus, Mozart had plenty of opportunities to contract endocarditis.

A new theory about the death of Mozart, pictured here, suggests that he may have contracted endocarditis, a serious type of heart disease.

Nothing Can Be Proven

In this excerpt from his biography entitled Mozart, German *writer and artist Wolfgang Hildesheimer comments on how easy it is for modern doctors to dream up new
medical explanations for the composer's death, all of them
possible but none of them, given the vagueness of the evidence, necessarily accurate. Hildesheimer also points out that
little is known today about how people living before the advent of modern medicine reacted to the physical stresses imposed by various illnesses.*

"For physicians, analysis of a medical history of the past is a
seductive [compelling] game with many possibilities. Yet it
can only be speculation, of course. Since nothing can be
demonstrated any longer, let alone proven, the researcher
can proceed to improve upon or refute the competing theories, according to his [own] evaluation of the material [sur-
viving evidence]. The result certainly makes informative,
often fascinating reading, but no interpretation can be bent
into a conclusive whole. Too many factors in the life and
death, not only of Mozart, but also of other figures from before the age of scientific diagnoses, justify the assumption
that not only the mind but also the body changes over the
centuries, at least in reaction to the varying conditions of life
[and therefore Mozart's ability to withstand certain diseases
may have been different from that of an average person
today]. . . . A sixteen-hour journey in a badly sprung coach
over cobblestones, or a banquet of fourteen overseasoned
courses [experiences which Mozart endured many times],
would do us in."

But having the opportunity to contract a disease is not the same
as actually contracting it. The important question is whether
Mozart exhibited clear-cut symptoms of infective endocarditis.
Since modern researchers cannot examine the composer's remains or study a detailed autopsy report, they must rely on old accounts of questionable accuracy or authenticity. In any case, based
on Mozart's alleged symptoms and medical background, a diagnosis of endocarditis does seem appropriate. According to William
Stafford:

Patients whose heart valves are abnormal, because of heredity or a prior attack of rheumatic fever, are especially prone to this disease; the infection lodges on the damaged valve. It can produce the symptoms Mozart is known to have had: fever, inflamed and swollen joints in hands and feet, immobility, vomiting and spots on the skin. Even today it can be difficult to distinguish by observation alone between infective endocarditis and a severe attack of rheumatic fever.

If Mozart had contracted endocarditis, it would explain not only his symptoms, but also his death. The disease is presently treated with antibiotics, drugs that fight bacteria. Without such treatment, it is almost always fatal. Endocarditis most certainly would have been fatal in 1791, since doctors lacked all knowledge of the condition and had no antibiotics in any case.

Bouts with the Bizarre

The diagnosis of endocarditis as Mozart's final illness is not entirely convincing because the symptoms of the disease are so similar to those of rheumatic fever. When medical experts examine the sparse, two-century-old evidence, they cannot be certain that it was one disease or the other. In addition, recent advances in medical knowledge and diagnostic techniques have revealed other, sometimes very complex and exotic medical conditions that can produce symptoms similar or identical to those reported by Dr. Closset.

One such exotic condition shows particular promise in solving the mystery of Mozart's death. Beginning in the 1980s, British medical researcher Dr. Peter Davies began to compile evidence for a diagnosis focused on another secondary illness that can develop following an infection: the Schönlein-Henoch (S-H) syndrome. Doctors believe that S-H syndrome, only recently recognized and understood, is caused by bacteria that enter the body in the course of an infection. Small clumps of these bacteria tend to lodge in the tissues of the legs, arms, and buttocks, which develop a purple rash as a sign of internal damage. The condition also causes high blood pressure, as evidenced by warmth, swelling, and tenderness in the joints of the hands, knees, and ankles.

In addition, S-H syndrome can produce symptoms such as severe abdominal pain and inflammation of the kidneys, which in about 10 percent of cases escalates into renal, or kidney, disease. If left untreated, renal disease can end in organ failure and death. Unlike earlier theorists who implicated kidney disease in Mozart's death, Dr. Davies suggests that impaired kidneys constituted just one of several complications of a specific and chronic condition.

In Dr. Davies's opinion, Mozart first contracted S-H syndrome in 1784 after a streptococcal infection or a bout with rheumatic fever. Some initial kidney damage occurred at this time. A second attack of the syndrome took place in 1787. The bizarre illness struck repeatedly between April and August of 1790, and each time the composer's kidneys suffered more damage.

According to this theory, somewhere along the way Mozart developed glomerulonephritis, a serious kidney ailment, as a secondary complication of S-H syndrome. This would be a case of one secondary medical condition giving rise to still another secondary condition. In glomerulonephritis, the kidneys swell up and become riddled with tiny scars. These problems interfere with the normal waste filtration functions of the organs and cause the body to retain water, salts, and nitrogen. The result can be renal failure, convulsions, and/or heart failure.

A Destructive Chain of Complications

According to Peter Davies, Mozart managed to avoid the worst effects of S-H syndrome and glomerulonephritis until his final illness began in November 1791. At that time, Dr. Davies maintains, a variety of medical problems combined to kill the ailing composer. First, he contracted a new streptococcal infection, which opened the door to S-H syndrome. This set of symptoms was accompanied by a worsening of the glomerulonephritis, which, when combined with loss of blood from venesection, brought Mozart's kidneys to the brink of failure. At the same time, the S-H syndrome caused his already high blood pressure to rise dangerously, leading to a cerebral hemorrhage, or bleeding in the brain. Dr. Davies sums up the causes of death in the following way:

> Mozart contracted yet another streptococcal infection while attending the [Freemason] lodge meeting on November 18, 1791, during an epidemic [of that common kind of infection]. The streptococcal infection caused a further exacerbation [aggravation] of Schönlein-Henoch

syndrome and renal failure, which [had symptoms includ-ing] a fever . . . malaise [weakness], swelling of the limbs, vomiting, and purpura [purple rash]. The later, more gen-eralized swelling of the body was probably due to addi-tional salt and fluid retention from renal failure. One or more venesections [bleedings] were performed and these would have aggravated his renal failure and contributed to his death. . . . His partial paralysis was a hemiplegia (paralysis of one side of his body) due to a cerebral hem-orrhage. About two hours before Mozart died, he con-vulsed and became comatose [unconscious]. Then, an hour later, he attempted to sit up, opened his eyes wide

Doctors of Mozart's time, like the one seen here, knew nothing about germs and other fundamental medical concepts taken for granted today; therefore, they often misdiagnosed their patients.

and fell back with his head turned to the wall; his cheeks were puffed out. These symptoms suggest . . . a massive cerebral hemorrhage.

This explanation of Mozart's death is certainly the most complicated and detailed ever proposed. It seems convincing, partly because it accounts for all the composer's reported symptoms. It also describes an increasingly destructive chain of medical complications caused and worsened by misdiagnosis, unsanitary conditions, and lack of proper treatment. The scenario, however, is consistent with the state of European medical knowledge and patient care in 1791.

Yet even this elegant hypothesis may not be the final answer. Some scholars have recently taken issue with several of Dr. Davies's interpretations of the centuries-old medical evidence. For example, Stafford points out that S-H syndrome usually affects schoolchildren; only rarely do people in their late twenties display its symptoms for the first time. Second, practically nothing is known about the composer's 1787 illness, and Dr. Davies's claim that it was an attack of S-H syndrome is no more than a guess. Furthermore, no strong evidence exists that Mozart suffered from high blood pressure at any time in 1791. These objections do not completely refute the theory, but they do raise enough doubts to keep the medical community from acknowledging it as conclusive.

The Disputed Skull

The latest theory for Mozart's death is also a medical one. In 1994 Ohio State University neurologist Miles E. Drake announced the results of his study of the composer's final illness. This investigator claimed to have identified the main culprit as a subdural hematoma, a mass of blood that accumulates in the narrow space between the skull and the brain. Subdural hematomas most commonly result from blows to the head, which trigger a slow leakage of blood, and it is suggested that Mozart suffered a head injury from a drunken fall sometime late in 1790 or early in 1791. But the composer did not seek immediate treatment and eventually he contracted an infection, perhaps streptococcal in nature. He then developed rheumatic fever or some other secondary illness and called in his physician. When Dr. Closset bled him, causing a sudden drop in blood pressure, the subdural hematoma became enlarged and brought on a stroke. This sudden and serious loss of blood to the brain tissues soon led to death.

The subdural hematoma theory rests partly on the scattered evidence of various medical symptoms and personality changes in Mozart's last year. First, Dr. Drake addresses what he calls the composer's "black thoughts" in that period. Supposedly, as the blood in the hematoma accumulated and dried, it put increasing pressure on Mozart's brain, explaining his mood swings, occasional depression, and paranoid-type fantasies about being poisoned. Dr. Drake also points to fairly frequent references in the composer's letters to headaches, which would be consistent with a blood clot inside the skull, exerting pressure on the brain.

The Drake hypothesis also rests on this neurologist's examination of what some people have claimed is Mozart's skull. According to science writer Josie Glausiusz:

> Although it has commonly been assumed that Mozart's remains were lost to posterity—like most folk of his time and station, he was buried in a communal grave—a skull reputed to be Mozart's was actually unearthed ten years after his death by the gravedigger who had interred [buried] him. . . . A few years ago the skull was analyzed by French anthropologists. . . . Wear on the teeth confirmed that the skull had belonged to a man between 25 and 40 years of age. And when the researchers imposed photographs of the skull on portraits of Mozart, they found that the skull's features—notably the high cheek bones and the egg-shaped forehead—matched perfectly.

Drake points out that the skull also has a small crack in the area of the left temple. Close examination reveals that the skull's owner died with the fracture only partly healed, indicating that no more than a year had passed since the injury. This, says Dr. Drake, confirms the idea that the composer fell and bumped his head, perhaps early in 1791.

The main problem with the Drake theory is that it hinges on two very questionable suppositions. The first—that Mozart had a drunken fall within a year of his death—is not supported by any direct evidence. The headaches mentioned in the composer's letters easily could have been attributable to other problems, especially considering his chronic illness. And his moods and depressions

Wolfgang Amadeus Mozart, whose untimely death, despite many exhaustive studies and intriguing theories over the years, remains unexplained and mysterious.

might just as well have been caused by money problems. Second, there is no proof that the skull with the fracture belonged to Mozart. It is likely that thousands of men between the ages of twenty-five and forty were buried in the same cemetery in the decade between Mozart's death and the gravedigger's discovery. Many of these corpses undoubtedly had high cheekbones, and at least some of the skulls might make a rough match with the composer's portraits. Moreover, since human remains were periodically removed from the cemetery to make way for new burials, it is possible that Mozart's skeleton was not there for the gravedigger to find.

The Mystery Endures

Thus, the newest theories, though fascinating and seemingly convincing, do not solve once and for all the mystery of Mozart's death. Endocarditis, S-H syndrome, and subdural hematoma must for the moment join company with other proposed explanations: that Salieri poisoned him; that the Freemasons murdered him; that rheumatic fever did him in; that he accidentally poisoned himself; that Dr. Closset bled him too much; that he succumbed to mental and physical exhaustion; or that depression and loneliness extinguished his will to live.

The sheer number and diversity of these theories only serves to underscore that the "facts" surrounding the composer's final illness and death are few, vague, and inconclusive. This invariably leaves them open to interpretation. Therefore, the mystery endures. Unless some dramatic new, unexpected, and definitely conclusive evidence turns up, the truth about Mozart's untimely end may never be known. As William Stafford puts it, the unreliability of the existing evidence may "always deprive us of the truth about what Mozart was like, how he lived and why he died."

For Further Reading

Roger K. Blakely, *Wolfgang Amadeus Mozart*. San Diego, CA: Lucent Books, 1993. A good general synopsis of Mozart's life; plenty of photos and reproductions of old paintings and manuscripts.

Hans Conrad Fischer and Lutz Besch, *The Life of Mozart: An Account in Text and Pictures*. New York: Macmillan, 1969. This general and easy-to-read summary of Mozart's life contains many paintings of the composer's contemporaries and photos of places he frequented in Salzburg, Vienna, Prague, and Berlin.

Charles R. Hoffer, *The Understanding of Music*. Belmont, CA: Wadsworth Publishing, 1985. An excellent, well-organized, and easy-to-read general introduction to the structure and history of Western music. Contains many references to Mozart and his works.

H. C. Robbins Landon, *Mozart and Vienna*. New York: Macmillan, 1991. In this fascinating book, the author describes the city and people of Vienna in Mozart's day and tells about the composer's experiences in getting and living there. Much of the book is devoted to a fine translation of German writer Johann Pezzl's *Sketch of Vienna*, published in the 1780s, which contains many interesting details about the customs, institutions, and artistic and musical works of European, and especially German-speaking, society of that time. Advanced but worthwhile reading.

Goddard Lieberson, ed., *The Columbia Book of Musical Masterworks*. New York: Allen, Towne and Heath, 1947. A very useful list of important musical pieces by Mozart and other great orchestral composers, with explanations and critical comment for each.

Ernest Newman, *Stories of the Great Operas*. New York: Garden City Publishing, 1930. This old but still useful volume contains good overviews of the plots of great eighteenth- and nineteenth-century operas, including Mozart's *The Marriage of Figaro, Don Giovanni,* and *The Magic Flute*. Important operas by other composers, such as Beethoven, Verdi, and Puccini, are summarized as well.

Michael Parouty, *Mozart: From Child Prodigy to Tragic Hero.* Translated by Celia Skrine. New York: Harry N. Abrams, 1993. A thorough, easy-to-read synopsis of Mozart's life. Contains many color pictures and drawings of people and places involved in the composer's life. A long and useful appendix presents complete documents by and about Mozart and his musical works.

Works Consulted

Emily Anderson, ed., *The Letters of Mozart and His Family*. New York: Norton, 1966. Rev. ed., 1985. This nearly 1,000-page-long source is invaluable to a study of Mozart, and nearly all modern biographers and Mozart scholars have quoted freely from it. All the letters—by the composer, his father, sister, wife, cousin, and others—are complete, uncensored, and footnoted to explain what now appear as obscure references.

Volkmar Braunbehrens, *Mozart in Vienna, 1781–1791*. Translated by Timothy Bell. New York: Grove Weidenfeld, 1989. This thorough and well-written examination of Mozart's last ten years of life includes discussions of his anonymous commission for the *Requiem*, his final illness, the cause of his death, and the circumstances of his burial.

Marcia Davenport, *Mozart*. New York: Charles Scribner's Sons, 1932. A lively, easy-to-read summary of Mozart's life that accepts and dramatizes the "mysterious messenger" story and also the idea that the composer ended up in a pauper's grave.

Peter J. Davies, "Mozart's Illnesses and Death," *Musical Times*, vol. 125, 1984. Dr. Davies goes into great detail about Mozart's medical conditions, examines the evidence surrounding the composer's last months, weeks, and days, and arrives at some new, very believable, and satisfying conclusions about his mysterious death.

Otto Erich Deutsch, *Mozart: A Documentary Biography*. Translated by Eric Blom, Peter Branscombe, and Jeremy Noble. Stanford, CA: Stanford University Press, 1965. This scholarly work is one of the most valuable single sources for a serious study of Mozart. There is no text in the usual sense, but rather, a compendium of primary source documents—letters, birth and death notices, newspaper reports, music reviews, diary entries, and so on—either by or about Mozart and those closest to him. Each document is accompanied by explanation and comment.

Alfred Einstein, *Mozart: His Character, His Work*. New York: Oxford University Press, 1965. This is a reprint of Einstein's 1945 study in which he suggested that Mozart was caught in an "eternal struggle between body and soul," a battle that led to illness, overwork, and death.

Josie Glausiusz, "The Banal Death of a Genius," *Discover*, March 1994. A summary of new findings by Dr. Miles Drake of Ohio State University suggesting that Mozart died from a subdural hematoma sustained after a drunken fall.

Wolfgang Hildesheimer, *Mozart.* Translated by Marion Faber. New York: Farrar Straus Giroux, 1982. A detailed modern biography of the composer, including much analysis of his music and also a list of his major works.

Edward Holmes, *The Life of Mozart, Including His Correspondence.* New York: Dacapo Press, 1979. A reprint of Holmes's biography, which originally appeared in London in 1845. It was one of the more important volumes on the composer's life in the nine-teenth century. This very scholarly work nevertheless passed along such questionable information from earlier biographers as the accusation that Mozart cheated often on his wife and that he and some friends performed parts of the *Requiem* on his deathbed.

H. C. Robbins Landon, *1791: Mozart's Last Year.* New York: Schirmer Books, 1988. A penetrating, scholarly study of Mozart's activities in the final phase of his life. The author surveys some of the main theories for the composer's death and ends up favoring that recently put forward by Dr. Peter Davies, namely, death by Schönlein-Henoch syndrome. Robbins Landon also offers an entire chapter on Constanze Mozart, defending her against various writers and critics who have, over the years, faulted her for mismanaging the household finances and for failing to offer her husband more understanding in his times of crisis.

Franz Niemetschek, *Life of Kapellmeister Wolfgang Mozart, According to Original Descriptions.* Prague: Herrlischen Buchhandlung, 1798. The first full-length biography written about the composer contains many passages and descriptions that later biographers and scholars accepted and copied, even though some of Niemetschek's information was based on hearsay and was, therefore, of questionable authenticity.

George Nobbe, "The Fall of Mozart," *Omni*, December 1994. More information about Mozart's supposed drunken fall.

William Stafford, *The Mozart Myths: A Critical Reassessment.* Stanford, CA: Stanford University Press, 1991. An excellent summary and study of the various theories proposed over the years for Mozart's death. Well documented with letters by Mozart and his relatives and friends; also contains excerpts from the many later writings about the composer.

Index

Abduction from the Seraglio,
13–14
Amadeus, 41–42
Arnold, Ignaz, 59–60

Bach, Johann Christian, 11, 12
Bär, Carl, 56
Barisani, Sigmund, 24, 51
Beethoven, Ludwig van, 38–39
Boissevain, Willem, 78
Braunbehrens, Volkmar
  on Mozart's achievements,
  60–61
  reveals anonymous patron, 37

Carpani, Giuseppe, 42
Chabot, Duchess de, 71
Closset, Dr. Thomas
  "bled" Mozart, 56, 79, 84–85
  gives cause of Mozart's death,
  34
  on mercury poisoning, 45
  misdiagnosed Mozart's illness, 52–54
  at Mozart's death, 29, 30–31,
  47–48

Davies, Dr. Peter, 81–84
death of Mozart, 29–31
  see also theories of Mozart's
  death
Don Giovanni, 15, 69
Drake, Miles E., 84–85

Einstein, Alfred, 62, 72
endocarditis, 78–79, 81

Freemasons, 43–45

gastroenteritis, 55–56

Glausiusz, Josie, 85
Gluck, Christoph Willibald, 11
Greither, Aloys, 54–55

Hasse, Johann Adolf, 11
Haydn, Franz Joseph, 11
heart disease, 78–79, 81
Hildesheimer, Wolfgang, 80
  on Mozart's mental health,
  72, 73
  on Mozart's physical appearance, 68–69

Idomeneo, 13, 72

Joseph II, 10, 14, 15, 69

King of Pontus, 12

Lange, Joseph (Mozart's
  brother-in-law), 73
Leopold II, 15, 69, 70
*Letters of Mozart and His Fam-
  ily,* 51, 60, 65, 66
Lietgeb, Franz, 37
Lobes, Guldener von, 52–53,
  54
Lucio Silla, 12

Magic Flute, 15, 25, 71–72
  Mozart's final opera, 20
  well-liked, 21–22
Marriage of Figaro, 15, 69
Mithridates, 12
Mozart, 80
Mozart and Salieri, 40, 41
Mozart, Anna Maria (mother),
  8, 72
Mozart, Constanze (wife),
  14–15, 63, 65, 74

cares for Mozart, 27, 29–30, 47, 56

following Mozart's death, 24, 31

  questions cause of, 35–36

  suspects Salieri, 42

  tries to publish *Requiem*, 38

at health spa, 22–23, 70

Nannerl and, 69–70

Requiem commission and, 19

Mozart, Franz Wolfgang Xaver (son), 15

Mozart: His Character, His Work, 62

Mozart in Vienna, 37

Mozart, Karl Thomas (son), 15, 34–35

Mozart, Leopold (father), 8–9, 10, 64, 72, 75

  death of, 15

  letters from son, 51, 60, 65, 66, 71

  records son's illnesses, 48–49, 51, 55

Mozart, Maria Anna Thekla (cousin), 64, 65

Mozart Myths, 43–44

Mozart, Nannerl (sister), 55, 67, 72

  Constanze and, 69–70

  on Mozart's immaturity, 63

  as musician, 8–9, 10–11

Mozart, Wolfgang Amadeus, 8

  burial of, 31–32, 44–45

  as child composer, 11–14

    first commission of, 12

    influenced by Italian composers, 12

  as child prodigy, 9, 10–12

  childhood illnesses of, 49, 50

  death of, 29–31

    by fever and rash, 34

    from effects of "bleeding," 56, 79, 84–85

    by jealous colleagues, 38, 40, 41

    by primitive knowledge, 47–48, 54, 79, 83, 84

    unreliable facts about, 36, 80–81, 87

  as Freemason, 43–44, 82

  final days of, 16, 29–31

    divine messages during, 27–28

  financial difficulties of, 14–15, 63–64, 69

    as young man, 12

  foul language of, 64–65, 66

  health of, 15, 18, 23, 47, 51

    divine explanation for, 23–24

    working on *Magic Flute*, 21, 22

  as husband and father, 14–15, 22–23, 65

  letters from

    to baroness, 65

    to colleague, 25

    to Constanze, 22–23, 71–72

    to cousin, 64

    to father, 65, 66, 71

  obituary of, 18

  physical appearance of, 61–62, 68–69

  professional rejection and, 13–14, 15, 69, 76–77

  Requiem commission and, 18–31

    commemorates his death, 28, 35

  sexual affairs of, 65

  unknown messenger and, 18–21, 25–27, 37

  unknown patron and, 19–20

    poisoning Mozart, 35

see also theories of Mozart's death

Niemetschek, Franz
on commission of *Requiem*, 18–20
on Mozart's death, 35–36, 67

opera house, 76

Parouty, Michael, 10–11, 63–64
Puchberg, Johann Michael, 63
Pushkin, Aleksandr, 40, 41

Requiem, 39
commissioned by, 37–38
consumed Mozart, 18, 28–31
rheumatic fever, 50
Rimsky-Korsakov, Nikolay, 41
Rochlitz, Friedrich, 36, 37

Salieri, Antonio, 13, 23, 38–42
confessed to poisoning, 38
Sallaba, Mathias von, 45, 53–54
Schenk, Johann, 22
Schlichtegroll, Friedrich, 61–62
S-H (Schönlein-Henoch) syndrome, 81–84
Shaffer, Peter, 41–42
Sly Maiden, 12
Sophie (Mozart's sister-in-law)
cares for Mozart, 29–31, 43, 47, 56
on Mozart's mental health, 73
Stadler, Abbe Maximilian, 37–38
Stadler, Anton, 28–29
accused of poisoning Mozart, 44

Stafford, William, 66, 87
on heart disease, 80–81
on Mozart as genius, 74
on Mozart's failures, 69, 70
on rheumatic fever, 50
on secret societies, 43–44
Süssmayer, Franz, 22, 38
before Mozart's death, 28, 29–30, 47

theories of Mozart's death
depression, 68, 69–77
as artistic rebel, 76–77
as tragic genius, 74–75, 77
disease, 33
endocarditis, 78–81
kidney failure, 52, 54–56, 81–82
rheumatic fever, 52–54, 56
S-H syndrome, 81–84
subdural hematoma, 84–86
exhaustion, 33, 58–62, 66–67
due to creative energy, 59
physical, 60–62
lifestyle, 59, 62–66
poisoning, 33, 34–46
by Freemasons, 43–44
by mercury, 45
by Salieri, 38–42
self-inflicted, 45
by unknown patron, 19–20, 35, 37
previous illnesses, 33, 48–51

Walsegg-Stuppach, Count Franz, 37–38
Weber, Constanze. *See* Mozart, Constanze

Picture Credits

About the Author

Don Nardo is an award-winning author whose more than seventy books cover a wide range of topics. A trained historian and history teacher, he has produced several historical studies in addition to this one on Mozart's death. These include works on the ancient world, Mr. Nardo's specialty, such as *The Roman Empire, Traditional Japan, the Battle of Marathon, The Punic Wars, Caesar's Conquest of Gaul, Life in Ancient Greece,* and biographies of Julius Caesar and Cleopatra. Among his books about modern history are *Braving the New World,* the saga of African Americans in colonial times, *The War of 1812, World War II: The War in the Pacific, The U.S. Presidency,* and biographies of Thomas Jefferson, Charles Darwin, and Franklin D. Roosevelt. In addition, Mr. Nardo has written numerous screenplays and teleplays, including work for Warner Brothers and ABC Television. He lives with his wife Christine on Cape Cod, Massachusetts.